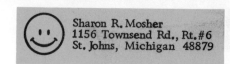

Creative Needlepoint Borders

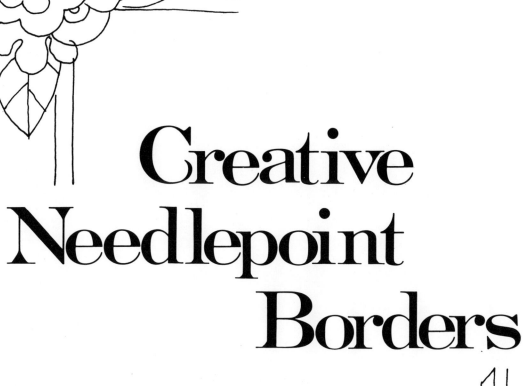

Creative
Needlepoint
Borders

MAGGIE WALL

Drawings by Barbara Eyre

Photography by Harold Pratt

CHARLES SCRIBNER'S SONS
NEW YORK

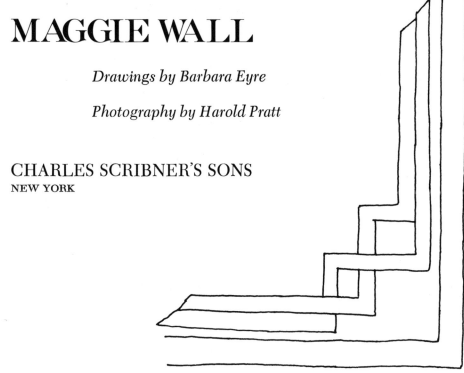

Library of Congress Cataloging in Publication Data

Wall, Maggie.
    Creative needlepoint borders.

      1. Canvas embroidery.   I. Title.
TT778.C3W33   746.4'4   76-46366
ISBN 0-684-14854-4

1 3 5 7 9 11 13 15 17 19 MD/C 20 18 16 14 12 10 8 6 4 2

Printed in the United States of America

*For W. W. W. with love and thanks
for your patience and understanding.*

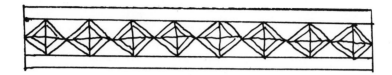

Acknowledgments

To those people who have given their time and ideas to the writing and execution of this book, I am more than grateful. I would like to express special thanks to the following: Barbara Eyre, my good friend and partner, who gave much of her valued time and talent to producing the line drawings; Harold Pratt, who spent many weekends and late evenings accommodating my requests for just one more photograph, and his wife, Edith, whose patience is seemingly unending; Gay Ayers and Muriel Baker, whose technical knowledge and stitching prowess would be hard to equal and who so generously shared their talents with me; Diane Mosely, who gave me the opportunity to renew an old friendship while toiling over a myriad of stitch graphs; Chottie Alderson, a new and valued friend, though we have met only through the media of reversible plaid, her very own invention; Ginger Tayntor and Bonnie Nathanson, whose sewing abilities and unique ideas in the mounting chapter were invaluable; Joshua and Pegge Missal, whose framing techniques and suggestions gave an added dimension to several of the needlework pieces; Edith Panaro, for typing and retyping the manuscript; and last, but not least, Hillary Wall and Leigh Eyre, two young girls who conspired to create a long-labored-over pillow to be treasured forever.

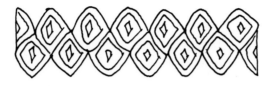

Introduction

Have you ever finished a piece of needlepoint and felt that it was lacking some finishing touch? This happened to me several times until I suddenly discovered that like a chef, adding a dash of this and a pinch of that to a special dish and turning it into a gourmet delight, I could add a border or an interesting corner piece to my needlework and turn each piece of ordinary needlepoint into a work of art.

There are many ways to complete your canvas work with a border, and several types of borders that may be used. The possibilities seem endless and indeed perhaps they are.

For the plaid and tweed enthusiasts, fabric designers over the years have created patterns that can be adapted to various forms of needlework. Charting your favorite fabric for a border can be a fun and challenging project. You can also coordinate your needlepoint to blend in perfectly with the decor of any room.

Time, or lack of it, is often a factor in trying to stitch your piece; you may have a deadline in mind. I find that the minutes and hours fly by when I am engrossed in an interesting project. To finish before that upcoming birthday or other due date is often an accomplishment in itself, with no time left to add a border. Do not despair! In that case a corner piece is always a possibility or the finishing touch may be added by giving thought to a unique mounting technique.

To become a needlepoint artist try using some of the ideas in this book in various combinations. The borders you create will be the personal touch on your canvas and will be enjoyed over and over again.

Remember, don't hesitate to experiment!

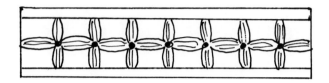

Contents

Mouline Border Sampler with small mirror insert in the center. Stitched by Lorraine Sandison.

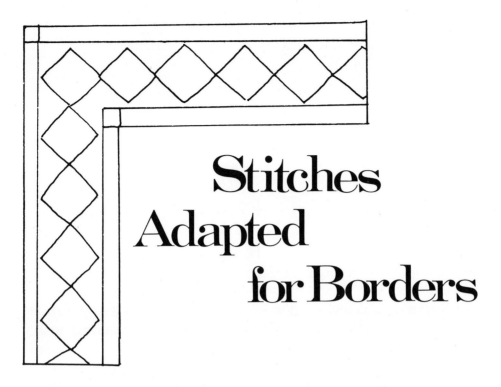

Stitches Adapted for Borders

The days when a needlepoint border simply meant adding a half inch or more in tent stitch in a contrasting color to the outside of a completed piece of canvas work are gone.

A border is defined as "a decorative edging, a design or stripe in the margin." On the following pages I will elaborate on this definition in order to inspire both the novice and the advanced needlepointer to exercise their imagination and ingenuity and create their own individualized borders.

Adding a border can be a rewarding challenge and will personalize your piece, but keep in mind that you must have patience and realize that canvas work can sometimes be quite unyielding and very demanding. Do not get discouraged Even the most accomplished needleworkers sometimes err and they, as you will do, simply try again.

I strongly recommend that all your work be done on a frame. It will hold your canvas taut, eliminate a great deal of blocking, and, when using more than one stitch, will keep the wavy, pulled look from occurring. There are many types available from art supply and needlework stores within various price ranges. For instance, there are artists' canvas stretchers, rotating frames, table models, and floor frames. Try to work on a frame at all times.

Work only on the best quality canvas, one that retains its sizing and does not go limp. There are many varieties on the market, both imported and domestic, and, at a glance, there is great similarity among several of them. Looks can be deceiving and it is not wise to purchase a canvas whose durability is limited.

Always keep an extra supply of needles on hand. They can be very elusive when dropped, and it is frustrating to have to stop stitching at a crucial point because of a lost needle. Dampness can cause a needle to rust. This will rub off on your wool, so make sure that your needle is clean before threading.

The time to plan and stitch your border is before you start your background. Most canvases you buy will have enough extra canvas on the outside of the design area, but if you are designing your own, make sure that you keep this in mind. Test the border you want to use to see whether or not it adheres to the border formula:

> Count the number of holes along the side.
> Divide by the stitch count in holes minus 1;
>   for instance, if the stitch takes 6 holes,
>   divide by 5.
> If this produces a whole number such as 99
>   or 34, rather than a fractional number
>   such as 33½ or 98½, the stitch will fit.

If you find that the count along the two adjoining sides differs so that one side is even and the other odd, move your outside line out a row or more on two parallel sides. However, before going ahead with this make very sure that your design is centered. If you are using a light-colored wool make sure that your stitch will cover the original outside line. If it does not, then paint out your line with white acrylic paint and put your new line in lightly with a no. 4 pencil or basting thread.

Another point about canvas to keep in mind is that when your border is complete and your piece ready to be finished you must stitch several rows of tent stitch around the outside of your piece. This is imperative. In the mounting process several rows are turned under and if they are part of your well-planned border you will lose the overall effect and many hours of labor will have been wasted.

The number of tent stitch rows required is a personal decision. Four is the very minimum whether your piece is to be made up as a pillow or as a picture. If your piece is to be mounted as a pillow, and your welting is to be incorporated into the border (Plate 10), four rows are adequate. But if you

A lovely Border Sampler done all in one color and
put to use as a pillow. Stitched by Marion Lewis.

really want your border to stand out do at least eight or ten rows of tent
stitch on the outside perimeter of your border (Plate 9). Plates follow
page 32.

Many border problems can be solved in advance by working up a
sampler of borders using stitches that appeal to you. Experiment with various stitch combinations. Such a sampler can be an invaluable guide for the
future and eliminate many catastrophes. Make more than one, each with a
different theme or color scheme; for instance, one in the muted tones and
one in the hot colors. Several such samplers are shown in the color section.

Another fun as well as useful project is to design your own pillow or
overall sampler such as the telephone–address book cover done in mouline
(Plate 1) achieving a striped effect whose stitches, when used separately,

create their own border. (See graphs, pages 17–24.) This will give you a good working knowledge of which stitches, when put side by side, can share a common hole and create agreeable patterns. Also, you can often combine two stitches that pick up the theme of your design (Plate 2). The leaf variation and Smyrna cross in two shades simulate the lily pad. (See graph, page 25.)

A piece for which you had no border planned and seemed to need that extra something will come alive with a little ingenuity (Plate 3). To enhance the Herb Pot design a combination of three stitches was used, the herringbone in wool, and the mosaic and cross-stitches in mouline. The floral with butterfly pattern is a good example of where it became necessary to move the existing outside line in order to use the cushion stitch as a border. The laid thread in this case was in a color that contrasts with the diagonal stitches so that the center of each set shows just a touch of another color: pink laid thread in the white set and white laid thread in the pink set. (See graph, page 25.)

Some stitches are more adaptable than others, need little or no compensating, and do not require an exact count. Some examples are:

Figure 1

Hungarian	Duck's feet
Persian	Encroaching Gobelin
Byzantine	Slanting Gobelin
Brick	Gobelin
Cross-stitch	Upright Cross
Jacquard	Milanese

Florentine and other Bargellos

Compensation is the act of making stitches fit together, against one another in a pleasing manner, into spaces not large enough to hold them.

You may want to miter the corners on some of these stitches. To do this simply draw a diagonal line from the inside corner of your border to the outside corner. Then start your work from the center of each side and work toward the corners (Figure 1). Also, the direction of your stitch can be reversed, and indeed sometimes should be, on the two sides (Plate 4, outside border).

CENTER
Star surrounded by diagonal tent.

CENTER BORDER
Parisian with mitered corners.

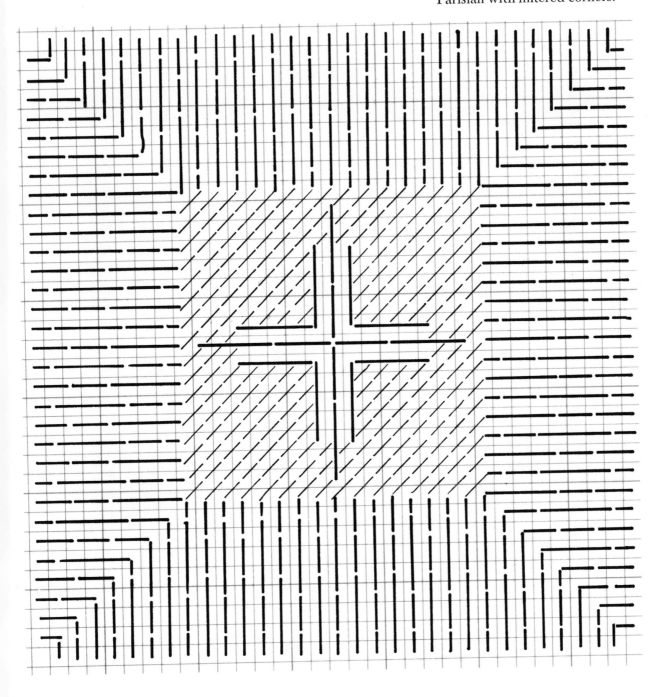

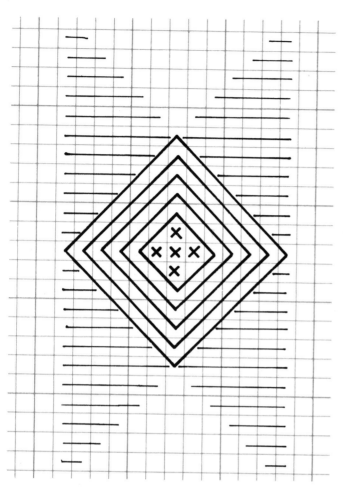

CENTER ROW
Brighton with princess filling. The Xs in the center indicate upright cross.

Stitches Used, Left Side of Center

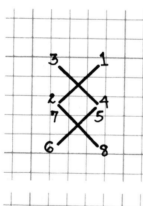

Cross over Three Holes
Come up on odd numbers, down on even numbers.

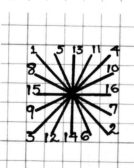

Double Leviathan
Come up on odd numbers, down on even numbers.

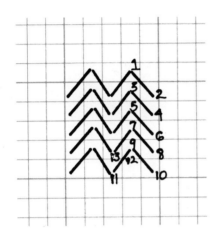

Kalem
Work from top to bottom, next row bottom to top. Up on odd numbers, down on even numbers.

Algerian Eye
Start at 1 and work around clockwise. All stitches go down in center hole.

Plate 1

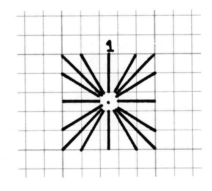

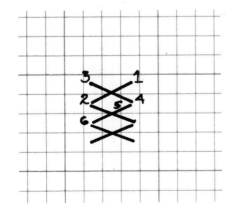

Czar
This stitch can be worked in two colors and gives a nice striped effect. Come up on odd numbers, down on even numbers.

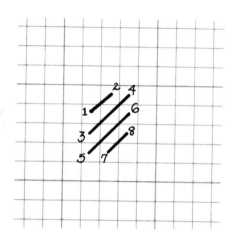

Cashmere

This is a variation of the mosaic stitch. Come up on odd numbers, down on even numbers.

William and Mary

Large diagonal cross (over three holes up and across) with small diagonal stitches at right angles across the arms of the large cross. The large cross may be worked in wool, the small diagonal stitches in silk or cotton. Two different colors may also be used.

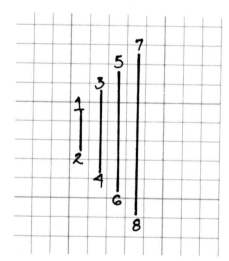

Groundings

A simple stitch where the second set fits in next to the first.

Smyrna Cross

A double cross worked over three holes.
First a diagonal cross, then an upright cross
over it.

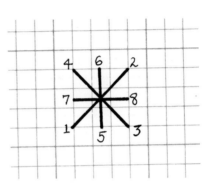

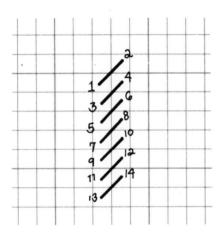

Continental Up and Down

Come up on odd numbers, down on even.
Worked from top to bottom, then bottom
to top.

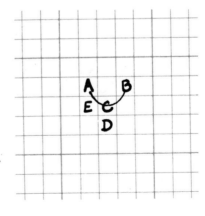

Closed Fly

Up at A. Circle thread in front. Down at B.
Up at C. Needle over thread. Down at D.
Up at E and proceed as above.

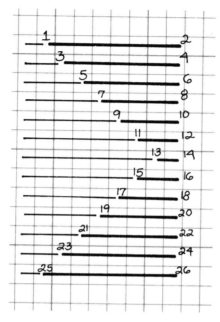

Straight Stitches

Fit second row into the first. Come up on odd numbers, down on even.

Plate 1

Stitches Used, Right Side of Center

Mosaic

Bring needle up on odd numbers, down on even.

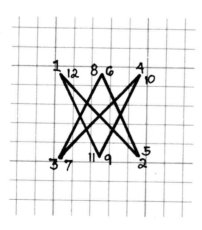

Triple Cross

Works better on #18 mesh. Up on odd numbers, down on even.

Plate 1

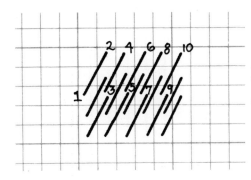

Encroaching Gobelin
Worked up three holes and over one. Gives a smooth texture.

Triple Diamond Cross
Do large X first. Then do the squares. Do small lines over the ends of the large X last.

Plate 1

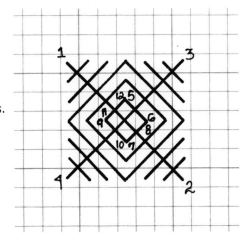

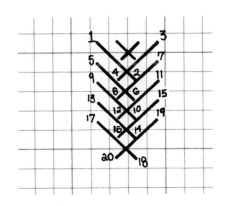

Fern
Thinner in appearance than fishbone, it also gives a striped effect. Up on odd numbers, down on even.

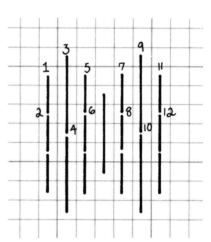

Hungarian

Worked over three holes, five holes, three holes, omitting a row, then repeat three-five-three. The next row fits between the first with short stitches under the long.

Plate 1

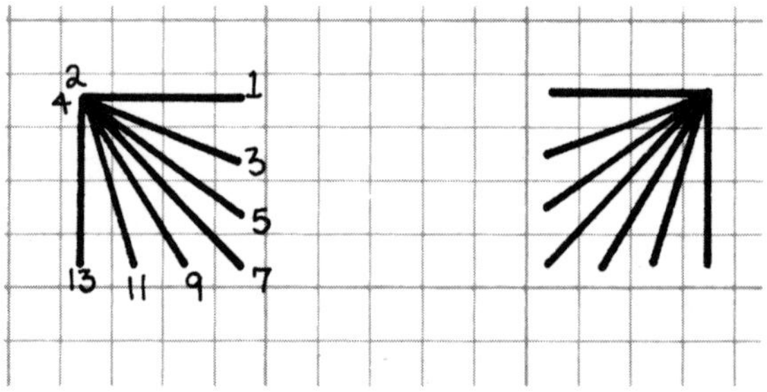

Ray Stitch

Can be done in either direction as the chart indicates. The two directions can be combined in the same row. All odd numbers occupy the same hole.

Plate 2

Refer back to Continental Up and Down, Closed Fly, Straight Stitches

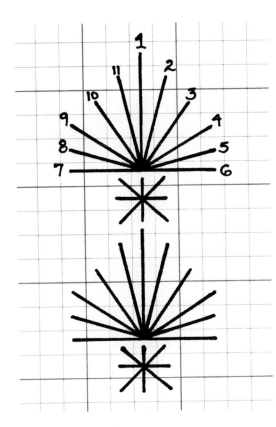

Leaf with Smyrna Cross

First stitch the complete leaf stitch with each stitch entering bottom center hole as indicated. Next work Smyrna cross underneath.

Plate 2

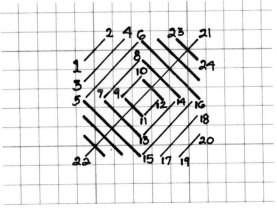

Cushion Stitch

Two "sets" of the diagonal stitches that form little squares. The second set is worked over a laid thread as indicated in 21 and 22.

Plate 3

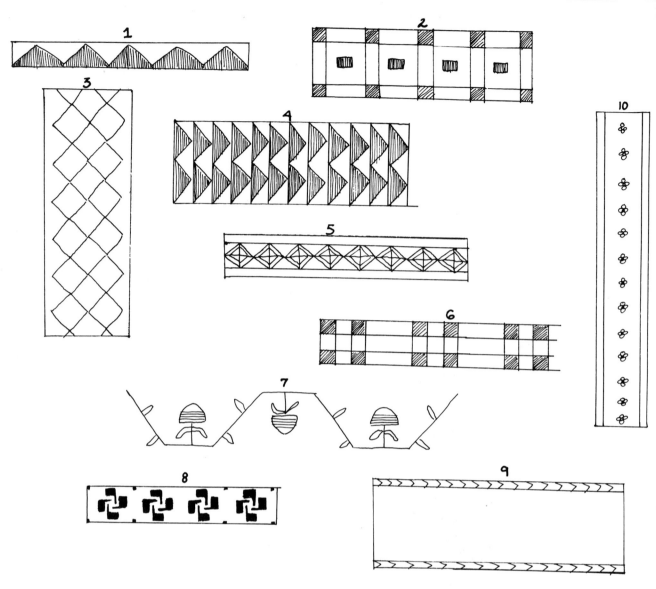

Figure 4, Plate 7 (see page 29)

Set 1–Upright Cross
    Straight Stitch 3, 4, 5, 6 holes
Set 2–Scotch Stitch
    Slanted Stitches and
        Straight Gobelin in center
Set 3–3-5-7-9 Diamond Surrounded by
    Brick and outsides 3, 4, 5, 6 holes
        Straight Stitch
Set 4–Van Dyke with compensation

Set 5–A crossed corners variation
    Cashmere
Set 6–Scotch
    Straight Gobelin
Set 7–Tent
Set 8–Tent and Slanted Stitch
    Tent going in opposite direction
Set 9–Long-Armed Cross
    Diagonal Gobelin

Often you will want to take the option of using a corner stitch (Plate 5, Set 3). Two stitches that can be used in this instance are Rhodes and Algerian eye as they can be made to fit any size, but I do not recommend enlarging these stitches to more than a 12 by 12 hole count. When the correct count allows, triangle and southern cross can be used. Other stitches, when used in sets to form squares, such as Smyrna cross, William and Mary, mosaic, and Scotch, also work out very well (Plate 7, Figure 4, Sets 2 and 6).

When choosing a border, particularly if you are going to use additional borders, make very sure that you adhere to the border formula. If the formula does not work, choose another stitch; compensating is not always the best alternative. A good example of this is the use of the fern stitch and diamond eyelet where the scene predetermines the border dimensions (see below). The Diamond Eyelet had to be compensated so much here that it distracts from the overall piece.

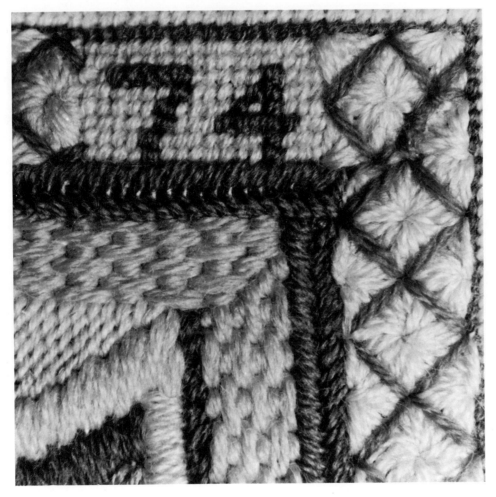

Incorrect use of fern stitch and diamond eyelet border.

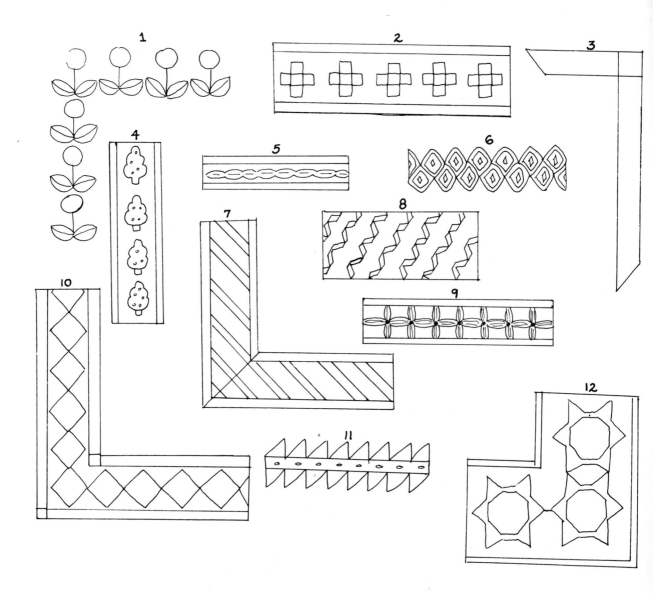

Figure 2, Plate 5

Set 1 –Spider Web
   Tent
   Diagonal Leaf
Set 2 –Smyrna Cross
   William and Mary in center surrounded
      by Algerian Eye
Set 3 –Tenny's Herringbone
   Rhodes Stitch at Corner
Set 4 –Tree with Red Beads
   Brick Stitch
   Cashmere
Set 5 –Oblong Cross
   Shell Stitch
Set 6 –Brighton Stitch

Set 7 –Diagonal Gobelin of varying lengths
   Duck's Feet border in two tones
Set 8 –Ribbon Stitch
   Tent Stitch
Set 9 –Rosemary and Beads
   Montenegrin Border
Set 10–Diamond Eyelet
   Straight Stitch
   Scotch Stitch
Set 11–Straight Stitch
   Oblong Crosses surrounded by Tent
Set 12–Milanese variations
   Brick Stitch
   Straight Gobelin

Sampler employing different mediums, with gold thread and mouline corner pieces added as finishing touches. Stitched by Betty Bohannon.

The wool border sampler (Plate 5, Figure 2) is an excellent example of how a composite of stitches can result in exciting effects. Beads can be a delightful embellishment (Plate 5, Sets 4 and 9), and the appearance of many borders can be altered by substituting silk, mouline, metallic, or other threads.

An otherwise subdued floral or nature design would most certainly blossom with the floret border in Plate 5, Set 1. A holiday design would be enlivened by the cheery Christmas trees in Plate 5, Set 4, or how about altering the colors in the tree motif to coordinate with a woodland scene? Another of the borders used in this sampler (Plate 5, Set 12) has been nicely applied in the turtle pillow (Plate 6).

Borders worked totally in mouline (Plate 7, Figure 4, page 26) have a rich, lustrous result which is often suitable for more elegant pieces. Mouline is a six-stranded cotton which has a sheen similar to that of silk, but is less expensive. Just make sure that when using mouline your threads lie flat. This is accomplished by stripping (Figure 3). The number of threads you use should correspond both to the mesh of your canvas and to the stitch being applied; it is important because if you use too many threads the stitch will appear bulky, and if too few your canvas will show.

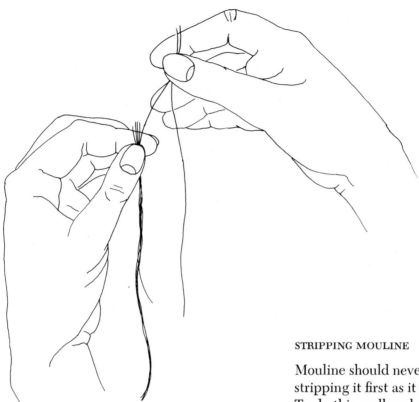

Figure 3

STRIPPING MOULINE

Mouline should never be used without stripping it first as it tends to twist. To do this, pull each of the six strands apart by holding them at the ends in your left hand, pulling each strand away with an upward motion. As each thread is separated, align the ends so that they are even and ready to thread in your needle.

This procedure takes a great deal of patience but is worth the time it takes in the ultimate result of your work.

Practically any stitch can be worked as a border. A case in point is the mice with cheese (Plate 8) in which the turkey knot was an amusing afterthought to a whimsical design. If you think a border can be worked, don't be afraid to try it and prove to yourself that it is or is not a possibility.

Borders and corner pieces provide the opportunity for you to become a needlepoint architect. Test your ideas on graph paper or canvas, and develop your own techniques. You will find yourself feeling more comfortable with some stitches than with others and you will become familiar with the various stitches and the patterns they make.

The incomprehensible when you are tired or frustrated will become more workable when viewed at another time or on another day. Try not to be careless, but if necessary remember that ripping out is not a waste of time; it will avoid disappointment later on. Poor work reflects on the doer and often will spoil a long-labored-over piece. Errors do not disappear, but rather become all too apparent and stick out like a sore thumb.

If, when ripping out, you cut the thread of your canvas, don't despair. It is not critical and can be repaired in a short time by applying colorless nail polish to both sides of the canvas where the break occurs. Let it dry, and when stitching make sure you do not use too much tension on that area. A better and more foolproof method is the following: Cut a small piece of canvas of the same mesh size. Place it underneath the broken mesh, lining up the holes. Using fine sewing thread, sew the small piece of canvas securely to the back of your work. This will not show when the piece is worked as the bulk will be on the back.

Butterfly Pillow showing placement of two corner pieces rather than the usual four. Stitched by Judy Zachs.

See graphs, pages 17–24.

Plate 1–Mouline Telephone–Address Book Sampler.
Designed and worked by Maggie Wall.

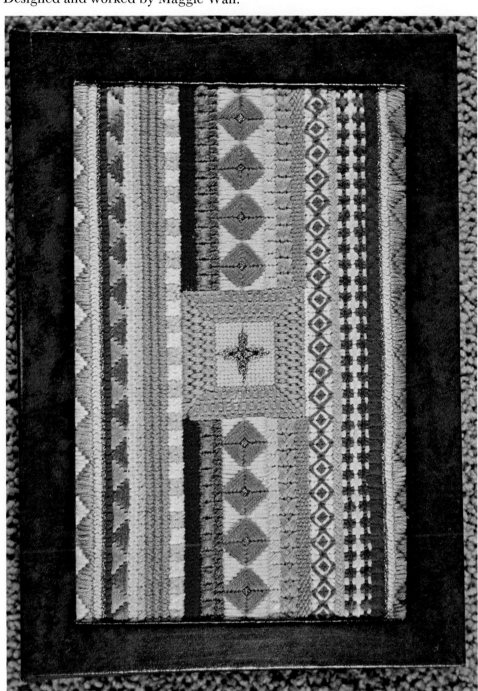

ORDER OF
STITCHES USED

Center

Star surrounded by
  diagonal tent
Center Border:
  Parisian with
  mitered corners
Center Row:
  Brighton with
  princess filling

Center to left

Cross over 3 holes
Double Leviathan
Kalem
Algerian eye
Czar—3 rows
Cashmere
Willam and Mary
Groundings
Smyrna cross
Continental
  (up and down)
Closed fly
Straight stitches

Center to right

Mosaic
Triple cross
Encroaching gobelin
  (5 rows)
Triple diamond cross
Fern
Hungarian
  (3 rows)
Ray
Continental
  (up and down)
Closed fly
Straight stitches

Plate 2–Frog on Lily Pad
using two borders: a
stitched inside border
simulating the lily pad and
a mitered ribbon border.
Worked by Jean Lincoln.
Designed by Barbara Eyre.

Plate 3–Two pieces of needlepoint which were
enhanced by the addition of stitched borders.
Worked by Belle Ribicoff and Maggie Wall.
Designed by Barbara Eyre.

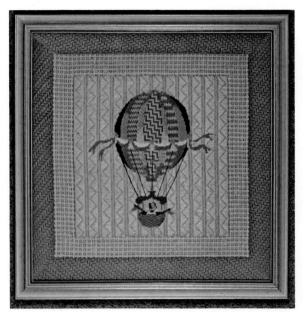

Plate 4 (Left)–Aerial Balloon stitched in mouline with pulled-thread inside border and Milanese stitch used in outside border with mitered corners. Milanese stitch is reversed on two sides. Pulled-thread border worked by Muriel Baker. Sampler designed by Barbara Eyre. Worked by Maggie Wall.

Plate 5 (Below)–Wool Border Sampler. Designed and worked by Gay Ayers.

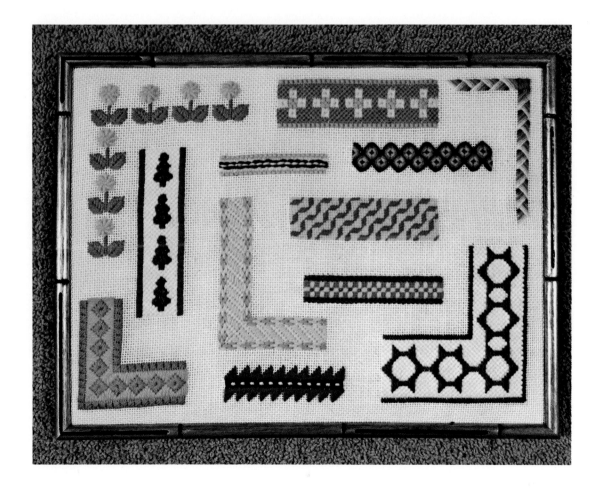

Plate 6–Charming Turtle Pillow using border in Plate 5, Set 12. Designed and worked by Gay Ayers.

Plate 7 (Below)–Mouline Border Sampler. Designed and worked by Gay Ayers.

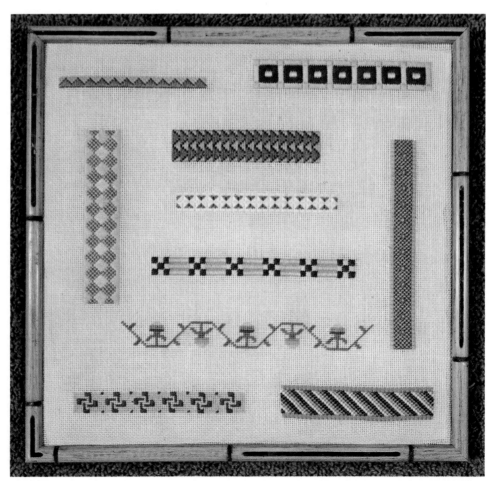

Plate 8–Mice with Cheese with Turkey Knot Border. Designed by Leigh Eyre. Worked by Hillary Wall.

Plate 9–Iceland Poppy Pillow. Ten rows of tent stitch were added outside border area so border would really stand out. Designed by Barbara Eyre. Worked by Maggie Wall.

Plate 10–Parakeet Pillow which was mounted to incorporate the welting into the border. Designed by Barbara Eyre. Worked by Belle Ribicoff.

Plate 11–Two clutch purses with Chottie's plaid as border and a small border piece showing "Chottie's Plaid Gone Wrong." Designed and worked by Chottie Alderson.

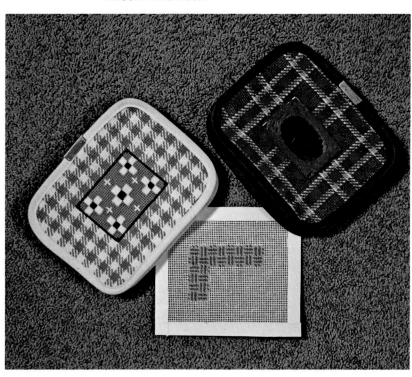

Plate 12–Corner Piece Sampler designed and worked
by Gay Ayers.

Plate 13 (Above)–Chinese Motif Pillow with geometric border which must be graphed before stitching (see graph page 58). Designed by Barbara Eyre. Worked by Jean Lincoln.

Plate 14 (Right)–Friendship Mice with Gingham Border. Designed by Barbara Eyre. Worked by Maggie Wall.

Plate 15–Egyptian Garden
Tray with various stitches worked.
in a painted border. Designed by
Barbara Eyre. Worked by
Maggie Wall.

Plate 16–Painted Border
Sampler. Designed by Barbara
Eyre. Stitched by Maggie Wall.

Plate 17–Pulled-Thread Butterfly with Narrow Chain Border. Designed and worked by Muriel Baker.

Plate 18–Curtain with tieback taken from flowers in curtain. Worked by Gay Ayers.

Plate 19–Matching tieback and pillow insert. Tieback designed by Joan Bobinski. Insert worked by Claire Bobinski.

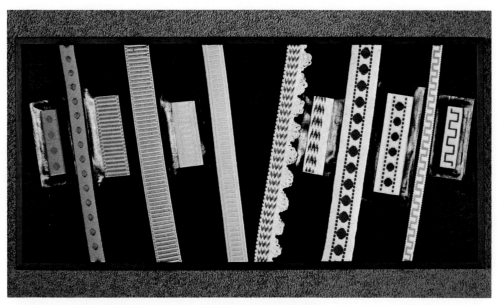

Plate 20–Border samples simulating fabric borders,
worked on #18 mesh. Worked by Maggie Wall.

Plate 21–Border samples simulating fabric
borders, worked on #14 mesh. Worked
by Gay Ayers.

Plate 22–Railroad Scene where railroad track
becomes the border. Designed by Barbara Eyre.
Worked by Maggie Wall.

Plate 23–Peaceful Lion with Fish and Stream Border.
Designed by Barbara Eyre. Worked by Beth Parson.

Plate 24–Game Bird Rug with garland of leaves and
berries which those birds eat. Designed by
Barbara Eyre.

Plate 25–Three Woodland Creatures with unique
painted borders. Designed by Barbara Eyre.

Plate 26 (Right)– Needlepoint Owl applied to ready-made pillow. Designed by Barbara Eyre. Worked by June Madden.

Plate 27 (Below)–Attractive pillow mounted with braid applied on top of mitered ribbon. Designed by Sunshine. Mounting by Bonnie Nathanson.

Plate 28 (Left)–Ruffled border creating a light, airy effect. Designed by Sunshine. Mounting by Bonnie Nathanson.

Plate 29 (Below)–Inserted pillow with ruffles to create a multi-border effect. Designed by Sunshine. Mounting by Bonnie Nathanson.

Plate 30–A good example of double framing to create
a border effect. Designed and worked by Muriel
Baker. Mounted by Grimshaw Gallery.

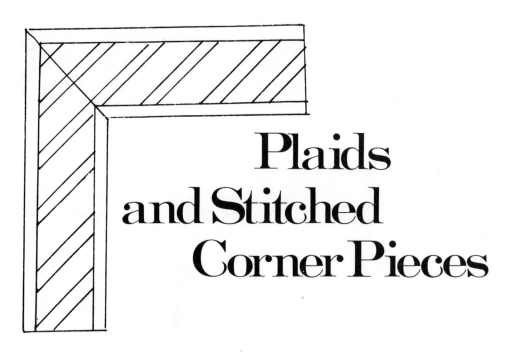

Plaids
and Stitched
Corner Pieces

Plaid in needlepoint has become known as Chottie's Plaid, because this reversible technique was originally planned and worked by Chottie Alderson. Once grasped, it is like eating peanuts. It gives the needlepointer a chance to use his or her resourcefulness, and you will find that it applies to any type of plaid you desire to re-create on canvas. It also opens up a whole new world of ideas for needlepoint borders that can be stitched in a relatively short period of time.

Having determined the count and colors for a particular plaid, it is just a matter of repeating the count and color scheme over and over.

Two clutch purses with Chottie's plaid as border and a small border piece showing "Chottie's Plaid Gone Wrong." Designed and worked by Chottie Alderson.

49

FOUNDATION

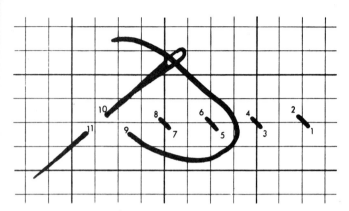

Diagram I

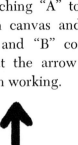

Determine top left and right corners of your canvas. Mark top left corner of canvas with "A" and top right corner with "B." Now note corners of this diagram page. Lay this diagram page on your canvas, matching "A" to "A" and "B" to "B." Turn canvas and diagram page (with "A" and "B" corners still matching) so that the arrow below is pointing up. Begin working.

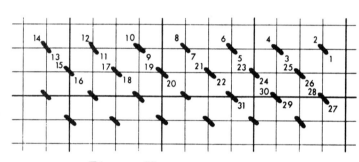

Diagram II

CROSS-HATCH

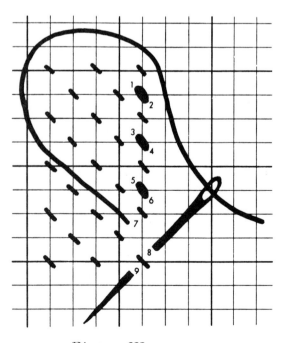

Diagram III

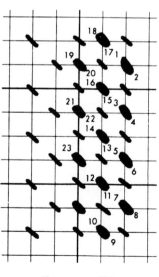

Diagram IV

How to Do Chottie's Plaid

To Lay Foundation

Follow Diagrams I and II, work 4 rows of color A, then work 4 rows of color B and then 2 rows of color C, staying in the same sequence of working *every other* stitch on alternate rows. Repeat this 4–4–2 count to cover the area you wish to be plaid.

Diagram I: method of working the stitch

Diagram II: rows of foundation worked

Note: Diagonal rows of *worked* stitches are also formed.

To Cross-hatch

Notice: "Cross-hatching" is filling in the unworked stitches that you skipped when laying foundation.

Following the same "A and B corners" directions, work with Diagram III and IV. Work 4 rows of color A, 4 rows of color B, and 2 rows color C. Continue in this count until you have finished the area.

Diagram III: method of working the stitch

Diagram IV: 3 rows worked

Be sure to check the back of your work occasionally as you work. It should look like the front except on the very edge or where you have tied on or off. It's easy to slip into working a regular continental (tent) stitch but, if you do, you have lost the whole ball game.

It is important to note that the stitches are worked in a nontraditional way: lower right to upper left. Follow the basic directions using the A–B corner directions on page 50. When the A–B corners are at the top of your work the stitches will lie in the traditional manner.

To create a tweed effect the same formula can be used by simply working a 1–1–1 count. Any number of colors can be worked; just use one row of each color and repeat the same count for cross-hatching.

To depict a houndstooth fabric use a 2–2 count and for gingham a 3–3 count.

As with other stitches, plaids should be worked out with some measure of prudence before actually being applied as a border to your piece of needlepoint. Make sure that a plaid will be compatible with your central theme and that you choose wools whose colors will blend harmoniously.

Figure 5. Corner pieces correctly applied.

Figure 6. Corner pieces incorrectly applied—too close to design, creating crowded effect.

It is possible to create a plaid border and at the same time apply your knowledge of other types of needlework. In Plate 11, different techniques were used in the centers of the two clutch purses: the Menzies tartan was stitched as a border on the blue purse and Chottie's plaid gingham was utilized as a border for the white purse.

The small border piece in Plate 11 is an example of "Chottie's Plaid Gone Wrong" and results in an interlocking ribbon design using the following count: 2 rows color A; 1 row color B; 1 row color C; 1 row color B; repeat. The two-count color is considered the background.

Corner Pieces

Corner pieces are another method of enhancing your piece of needlework and are less time consuming than a complete border. There are limitless possibilities, but they must be approached with conviction and an open mind. Don't let yourself get carried away and add a corner piece that makes the finished effect look too ornamental or obtrusive. A good corner design takes careful planning and sometimes restraint is necessary. Not all canvas designs are suitable to be used with corner pieces, and you must make sure that your corner piece is not misapplied (see Figures 5 and 6).

The placement of corner pieces is of utmost importance. It is not always necessary to apply them to the very edge of your background. They can be brought in close to the design and the background continued beyond how-

Figure 7

ever far you feel is necessary (Figure 7). This is an individual decision, but the structure of your design should indicate to you where to place the corner pieces and whether or not to apply them to all four corners or just the top two.

Corner pieces, unlike complete borders, can be started where the 90-degree angle is formed and worked to the edge (Figure 8). Rounded corner pieces such as in Plate 12, Figure 9, Set 12, on the other hand, should be started at the ends (Figure 10). The sampler in Plate 12 shows several examples of ideas that can be utilized in various combinations to give your piece a more finished appearance.

Figure 8

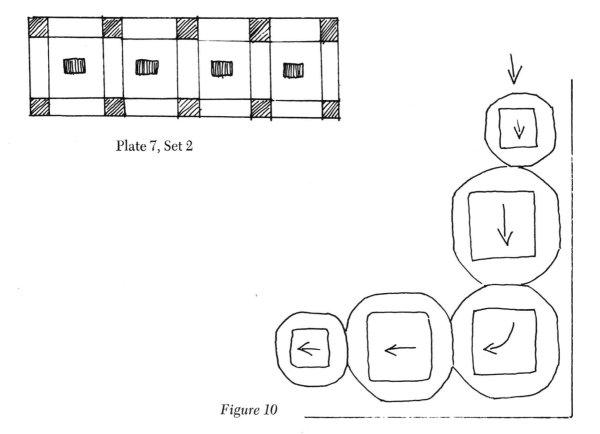

Plate 7, Set 2

Figure 10

Use colors in your corners which pick up the colors of your central design, and remember that there are limitations in terms of stitches. Those that form squares, such as mosaic, Scotch, banded cross, and others, adapt very easily. Be inventive and experiment with different shapes; the intermingling of various stitches can often produce the unexpected.

To find ideas for corner pieces look at magazines and newspapers, upholstery fabrics, rugs, china, and the items surrounding you every day. The design in Plate 7, Set 2, was adopted from the fabrics in a man's patchwork pants. Keep your eyes open—an idea could be right at your fingertips.

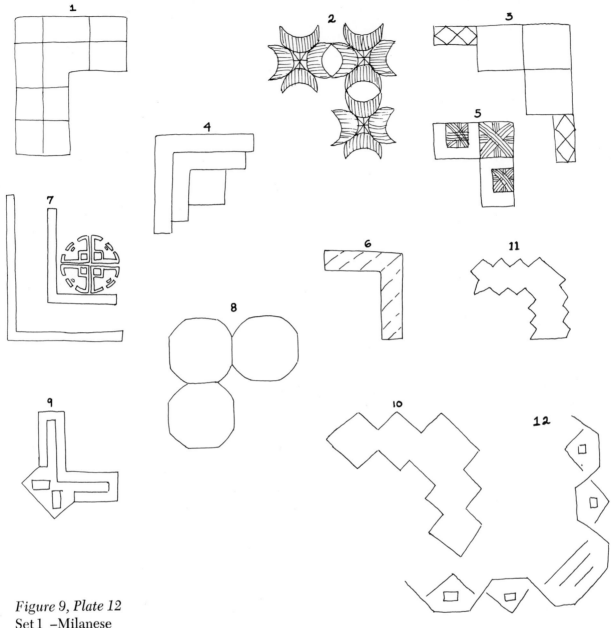

Figure 9, Plate 12

Set 1 –Milanese
        Slanted Stitch
        Smyrna Cross
Set 2 –Double Star
        Brick Stitch
Set 3 –William and Mary
Set 4 –Banded Cross
Set 5 –Rhodes Stitch
Set 6 –Cross Corner Variation
Set 7 –Flat Stitch
        Straight Gobelin
        Tent Stitch
        Mosaic

Set 8 –Scotch Stitch
        Straight Gobelin
        Back stitch–Single Strand
Set 9 –Mosaic Stitch
Set 10–Shadow Mesh
        Straight Stitch over 5 holes
Set 11–Diamond Ray
Set 12–Mosaic Stitch

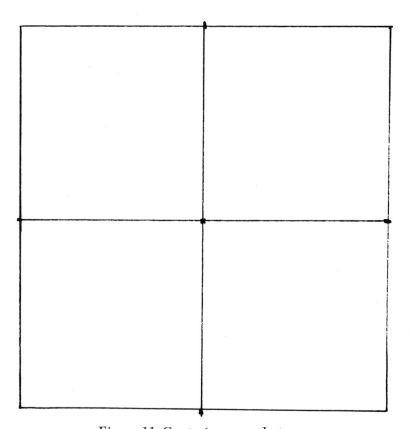

Figure 11. Centering your design.

Painted Borders and Corner Pieces

There are many instances when it is necessary to paint in your border. Do this before beginning to stitch your central design; it would be calamitous to inadvertently spill any paint on an area already stitched.

A painted border should be designed at the same time as the central theme, but if you are not the original designer this is your chance to give a piece your personal touch. A weak design can gain strength from a border, but at the same time an already strong design can lose its effectiveness and become too busy. Keep this in mind before making a final border decision.

When the border design is a geometric one and must be counted out stitch by stitch so that the corners all coincide and mesh correctly, it must first be done on graph paper (Plate 13, see graph, page 58). Be sure the design is centered before transferring your border to the canvas. To do this, first measure the outside dimensions of your design area, then find the center of each side and draw a pencil line forming a cross where the lines join (Figure 11). Start your border at the center of each side and work to the corners.

To achieve a gingham effect, a border made up of an exact count of squares looks easy but can be frustrating and very time consuming. The end result, however, is most gratifying. The Friendship Mice (Plate 14, Figure 12) would not exude half the charm if it were not bordered in this manner. Note that where the border meets the background the squares are compensated to fit. A variation of Scotch stitch was applied here; it is a good stitch to use when working a checkered pattern.

Painted borders allow the artist more freedom than do stitched borders, and depending upon the theme of your central design, your border can be simple or complex. The painted area need not always be of an exact count to

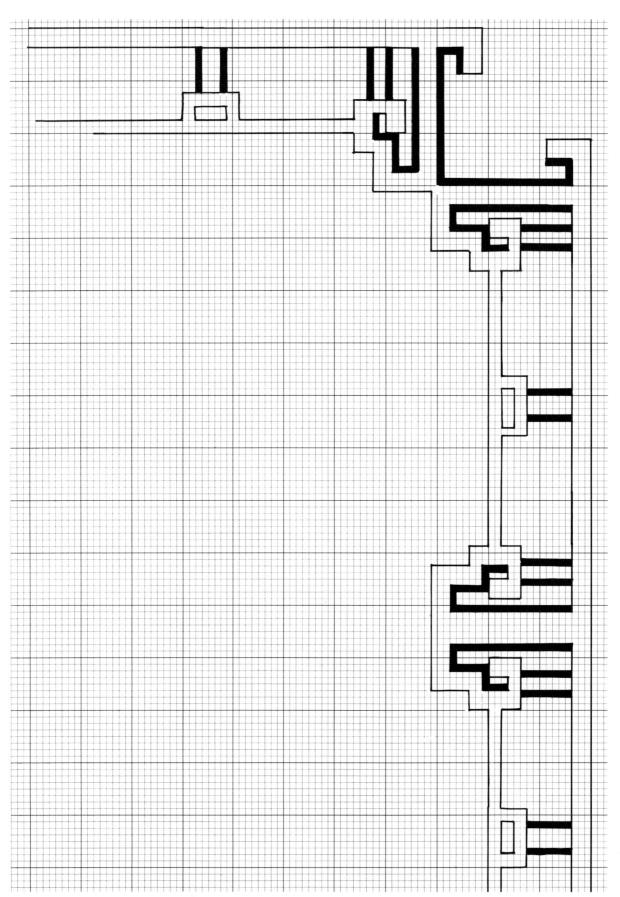

See Plate 13, page 40.

Figure 12

A–Variation of Scotch Stitch
B–Turkey Knot
C–Encroaching Gobelin
D–Upright Cross
E–Kalem
F–Cross Stitches
G–Brick
H–French Knots
 I–Parisian
 J–Straight Stitch
Rest in tent stitch

Figure 13

Set 1–Tent Stitch—outside
    Brick Stitch Sideways—center
Set 2–Scotch Stitch—outside
    Diamond Eye—Flower center
    Encroaching Gobelin—Pink Flower
    Cross Stitch—Yellow Flower
    Tent Stitch—Leaves and border
Set 3–Smyrna Cross at Corner of Square
    Overlay—Sides of Square
    Two Borders in Tent with row of
        Smyrna Cross between

Set 4–Tent Stitch
Set 5–Tent Stitch
    Dots in Cross Stitch
Set 6–Tent Stitch
Set 7–Gobelin over 3 threads, surrounded by
        sideways Gobelin over 1 thread for
        outside border
    Gobelin over 2 threads surrounded by
        sideways Gobelin over 1 thread for
        inside border
    Tent Stitch for background.

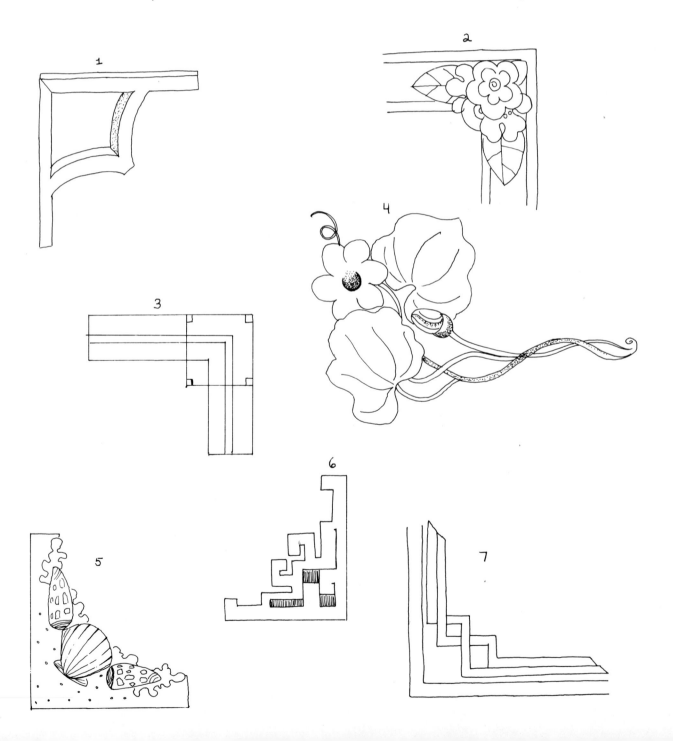

be effective. The Iceland Poppies (Plate 9) have a freehand border which has a spontaneous feeling to it, and yet it was not painted with an exact count in mind. This freehand approach is the simplest one, but it often dismays the perfectionist. If the result of your work pleases you, then don't try to elaborate upon or alter it. Above all, don't fret at the inexactness of designs done on a curve. Canvas work is flexible in many ways, and the curve is a point in fact.

The colors you choose are of prime importance. By picking up one or two from your design you are more likely to achieve an interrelated effect, but you can also use several shades of a nonpredominant color from your central design.

It may be that you will not want to paint a border on your canvas, and there is no reason to do so provided a simple border is chosen and you know what shades you wish to use and where. Simply outline your design with a light-colored waterproof marker and stitch it in with congenial colors. If, however, there is any uncertainty lurking in your mind as to the end result, painting the canvas can erase these doubts and will also clarify how your aggregate piece will appear.

Various stitches can be incorporated into painted borders and corner pieces and you may even want to design one with some of your favorite stitches in mind. A design you have purchased may already have a painted border in which you can incorporate different stitches such as the Egyptian Garden Tray in Plate 15.

Painted corner pieces, again, should relate to your central design. They can be tricky to apply, and each one must be carefully designed so that its size and shape coordinate rather than distract. Placement is an important factor in their success.

Types of painted corner pieces vary and they work up much more rapidly than a complete border. The sampler in Plate 16 and Figure 13 shows a variety of applications, each with a totally different concept.

You may wish to incorporate your corner piece into your border (Plate 16, Sets 1, 2, 3, and 7) or place your corner piece designs in two corners

Figure 14

rather than the usual four. Your analysis of placement as well as your perceptive ability will alter as your knowledge increases.

Some complex design ideas and techniques require more artistic ability to create than others. Don't be deterred if you have an idea in mind but cannot seem to develop it; you will surely find a friend who can help you out in time of need.

Elaborate corner pieces should be sketched out on paper first (Plate 16, Sets 2, 4, and 5). When your mental image has been formulated to your

Figure 15

satisfaction, both in size and theme, on paper, make a simple black ink outline drawing of it on either white paper or tracing paper. (If you use tracing
paper, put a sheet of white paper underneath it or pattern won't show.)

Put your canvas down on top of your inked drawing, and carefully
trace onto the canvas with India ink. Details of your original drawing can
be added when you apply your paint or as you are stitching. Figures 14 and
15 show how Sets 4 and 5 in Plate 16 were used to achieve a most effective
result using this technique.

A pair of lovely florals
with counted striped
borders. Designed by
Barbara Eyre.

Painted mirror frame border, suitable for child's room. Designed by Barbara Eyre.

Aerial Balloon stitched in mouline with pulled-thread inside border and Milanese stitch used in outside border with mitered corners. Milanese stitch is reversed on two sides. Pulled-thread border worked by Muriel Baker. Sampler designed by Barbara Eyre. Worked by Maggie Wall.

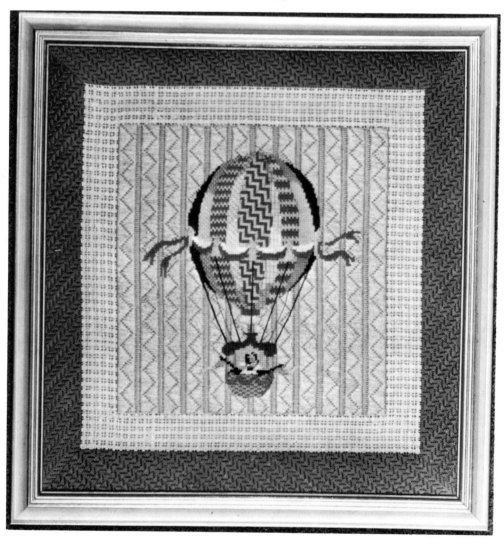

Pulled-Thread Borders

Pulled-thread work is an early English technique which when applied to canvas is very delicate and ornamental. It works up quickly and can give a fresh dimension to your work.

The terms pulled thread and drawn thread are often confused. The latter requires the actual extracting of the canvas threads to create an openwork ground before stitching. When referring to pulled thread, I am alluding not to this technique, but rather to the procedure of pulling your thread taut to create a variety of patterns.

Pulled-thread stitches combine very well with conventional ones, and many of the stitches used are the same as those used in other canvas work. The basis of all pulled-thread work is the tension of your stitch. When two stitches are combined to form a pattern, one stitch might be slack and another tight (see photo, page 68, and Figure 16).

Use a quality canvas and avoid synthetics, such as plastic canvas, at all times. Plastic canvases and interlocking canvases will not work as they do not have enough give and your thread will break when you pull.

Select a thread of hardy fiber, preferably mouline or silk. A quality brand of Persian wool is always acceptable and a strong metallic thread such as Schurer offers another option. Like silk, however, it can be costly and must be handled with extreme care as it tends to ravel and break.

Should one of your threads break . . . weep. Then rip back to a spot where there is length enough to run under. Unless the thread is securely run through on the back, a new thread will pull out as soon as tension is applied. To avoid this, start a new thread by making a loop after your first run under, put your needle through it, and run under again.

Pulled-thread sampler. Designed and worked by Muriel Baker.

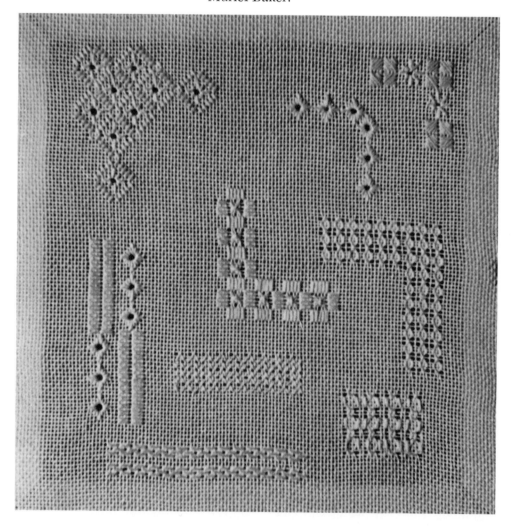

The graphs for these stitches begin on page 71.

Figure 16

Set 1–Diagonal with Center Star
Set 2–Diamond Eyelet
Set 3–Scotch Stitch with Star
Set 4–Ribbon with Diamond Eyelet

Set 5–Four-Sided Cross—Pulled Center
Set 6–Four-Sided over Three
Set 7–Reverse Tent
Set 8–Duck's Feet
Set 9–Four-Sided with Two Pulled Sides

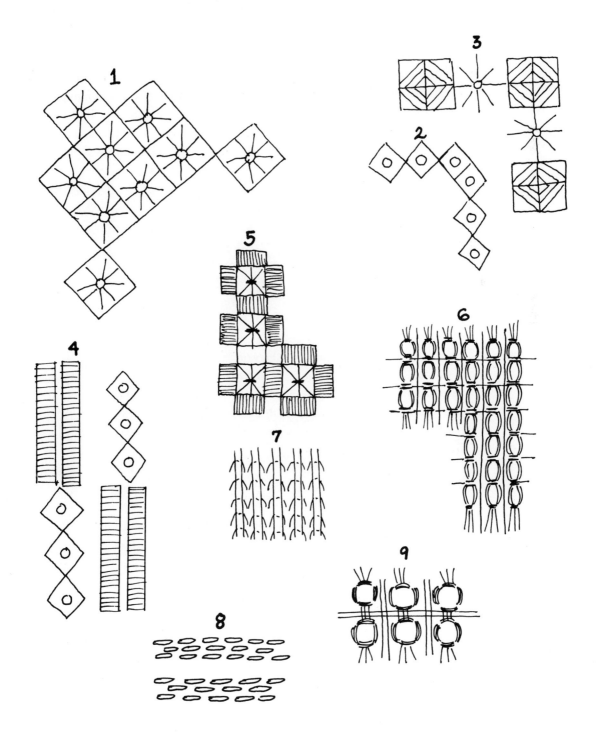

The number of strands you use depends first on the mesh of your canvas and secondly on the pattern and desired effect. When using silk or mouline, you would normally use a four- or six-strand count.

Be sure not to twist your thread. Minor twists seem to become exaggerated and stand out more clearly as your work progresses. Mouline tends to twist and should never be used without stripping it first (Figure 3, page 30).

The color of your canvas is another important aspect of pulled-thread work as the canvas does show. A monochromatic design gives the most pleasing results and pale threads that match the canvas will complement your work to the best advantage.

Should you desire to use a darker shade of thread, then it is necessary to tint the canvas. Before you begin your work, dye your canvas with a colorfast dye; or apply to the canvas area an acrylic or other permanent paint that is the same color as the thread you have chosen.

In order for the patterns to appear on canvas properly, it is essential to follow directions. If you don't adhere to the numerical order, your composition will show startling unwanted changes.

Exceptional care must be taken not to cross pulled holes on the reverse side of your work as they will show up on the front.

Charts do not always indicate the end result of a stitch in pulled-thread work (Figure 27 and photo,page 71).More often than not you will be surprised at the dissimilarity between the chart and your finished piece, so it is best to work up a few samples before applying them. Sets A and B on the right side of the photo show stitches from the same chart, but Set A was not pulled and Set B was.

Generally, in pulling threads, vertical stitches are pulled from bottom to top—i.e., come into the bottom and pull up. Horizontal stitches pull from left to right.

Most of the border suggestions and rules given in the first chapter are relevant to pulled thread. Follow the formulas and always start in the center and work to the corners on each side. It is easy to invent your own patterns by combining or rescaling stitches. You may also want to try combining a stitched border with a pulled-thread border (Plate 4).

The butterfly (Plate 17) is an excellent example of pulled-thread work, and the narrow chain border was a suitable choice for such a delicate piece.

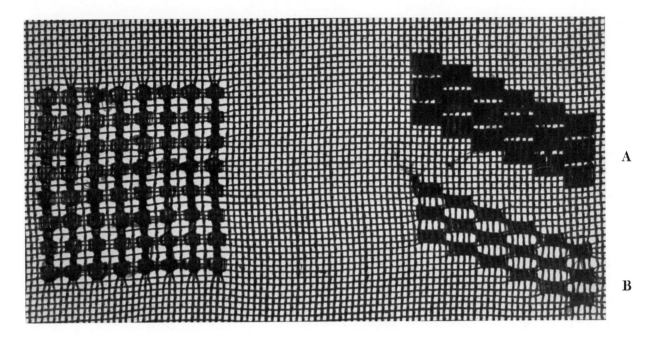

Figure 27

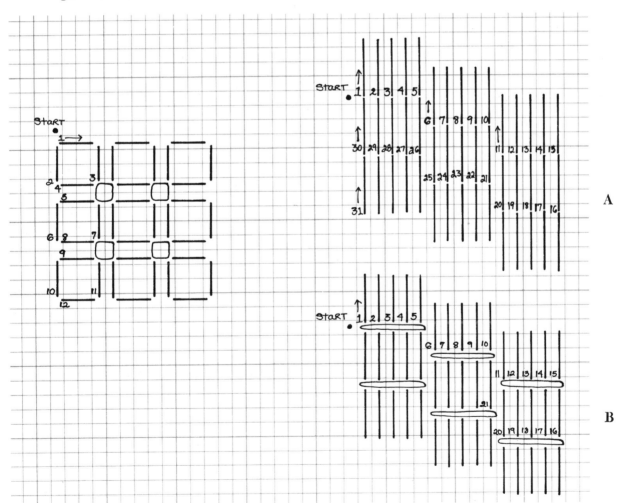

Diagonal with Center Star

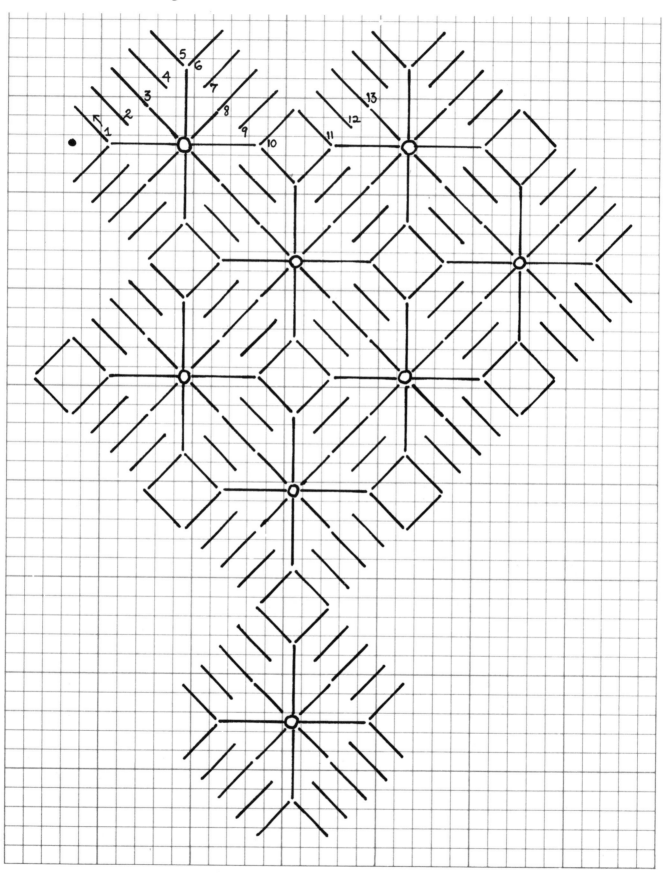

Five-Point Star: Diamond Eyelet

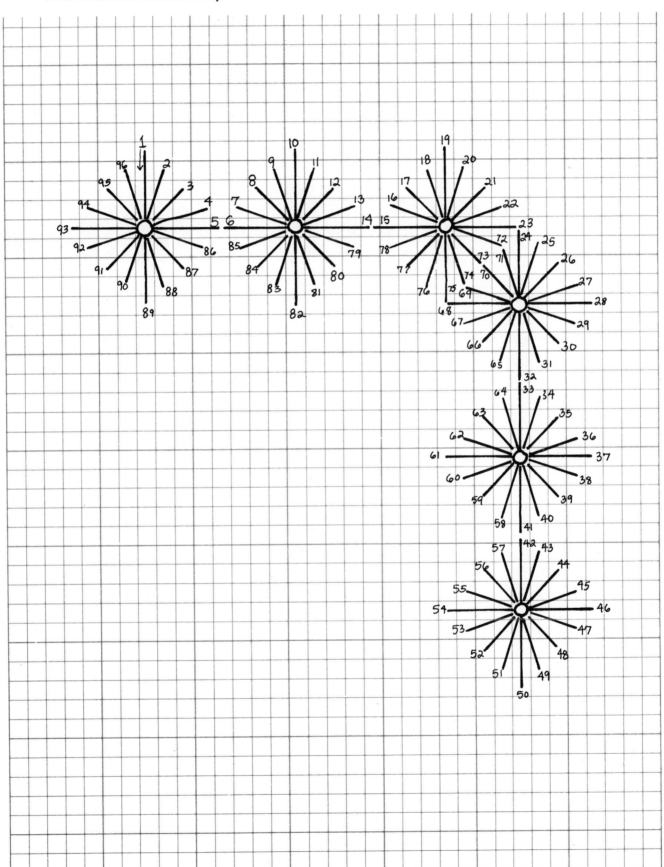

Scotch Stitch with Star

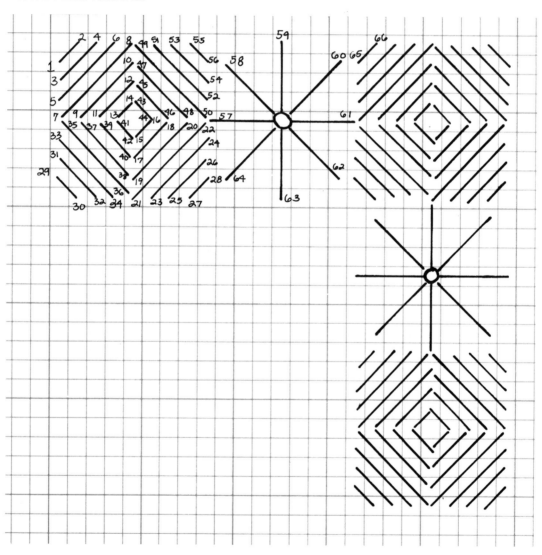

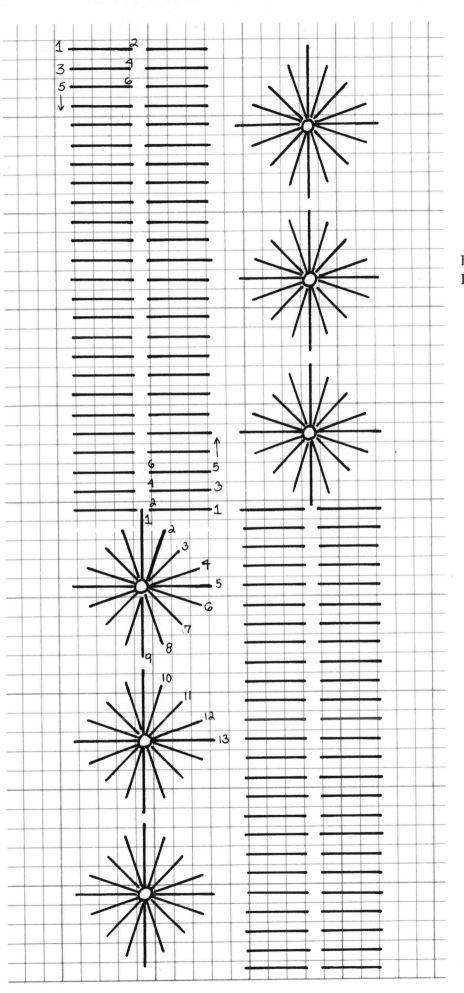

Ribbon with
Diamond Eyelet

Four-Sided Cross, Pulled Center

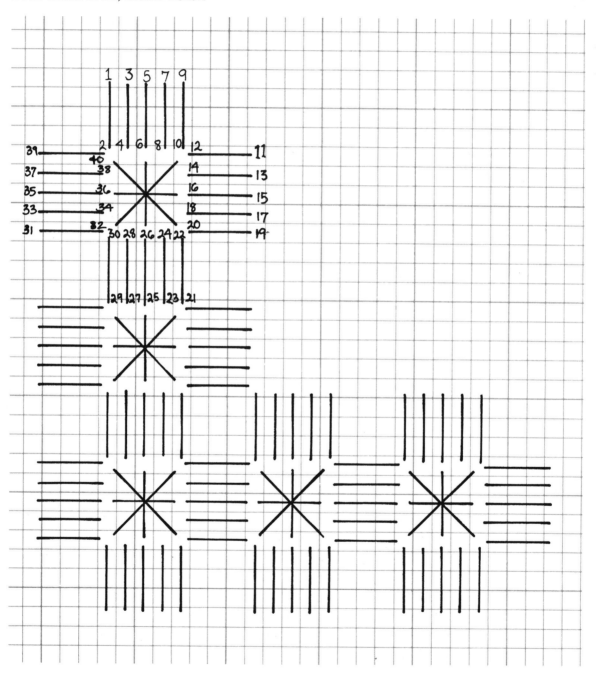

Four-Sided over Three

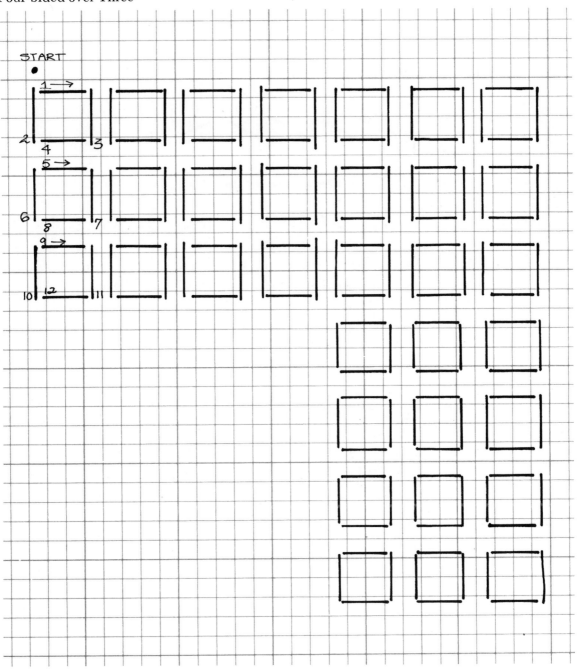

Reverse Tent

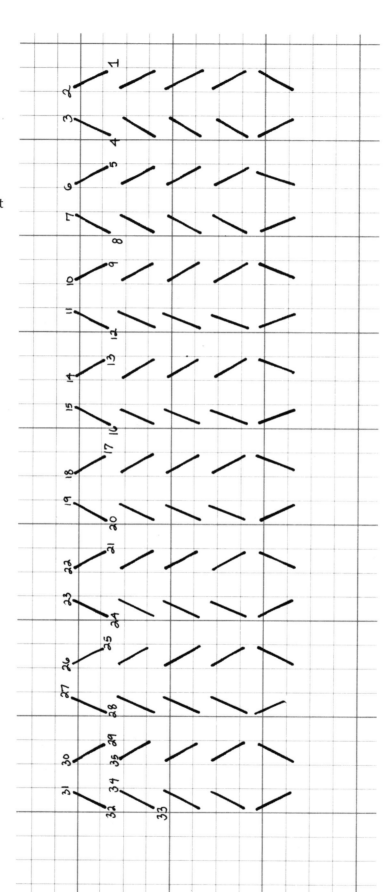

Duck's Feet

Four-Sided with Two Pulled Sides

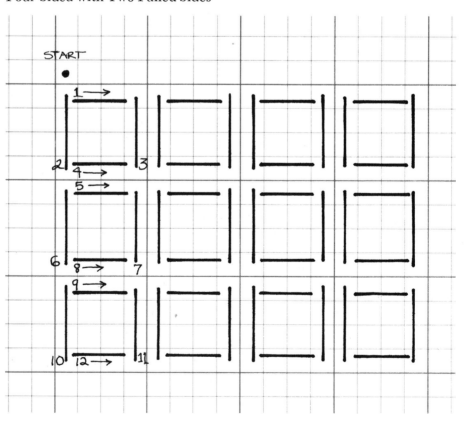

Pulled-Thread Pillow. Pulled-thread corner pieces and a mouline border combine with eyelet ruffle to create a dainty effect. Worked by Betty Bohannon.

Wool Border Sampler. Designed and worked by
Gay Ayers.

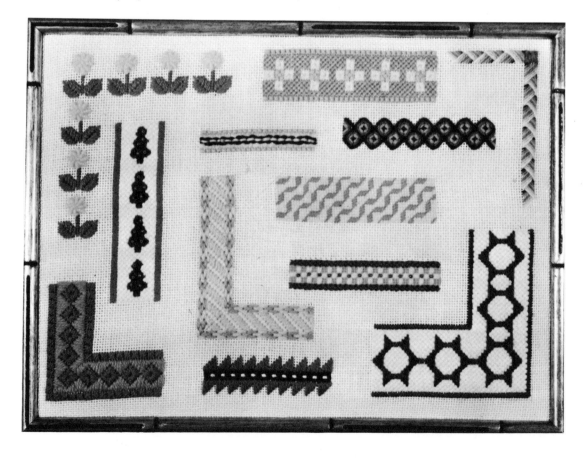

Coordinated Fun Borders

Coordinated borders, to me, are the most fun because they require the use of your imagination with a needle and a paintbrush. Thus, they fall into two separate categories; coordinating to reproduce fabric and coordinating to match the central design of your canvas.

Coordinating to reproduce the design from fabric is not easily done from every piece of fabric, but I have found that a vast majority of the fabrics do lend themselves to this method.

If your chosen material, and it may be one already in your home, on a chair, sofa, or bedspread, is either a print or has a repeat design, find a portion of the fabric design that can be reproduced on canvas. An example of this is the partially stitched floral border which has been duplicated from two of the small flowers in the curtain material (Plate 18). This border could now be used as a tieback for the curtains, as shown, or mounted on a pillow either in strips or as a border with mitered corners (Figures 17 and 18).

The curtain and pillow in Plate 19 are excellent examples of how you can apply your creativity to the interior design of a room. In this case the rich-looking moiré curtain is tied back with a coordinated needlepoint piece worked in a unique bargello design. The shades of wool used for the tieback have again been implemented in a floral inset for the matching moiré pillow. Both easily blend with the wallpaper and other fabrics in the room. When you are considering a decorating project, keep these ideas in mind.

Simulating the texture or design from material can all be done in tent stitch, but you also have the option of using a variety of stitches. You may want to graph them, although I prefer to experiment on scraps of canvas so that I can really see the results as I go along.

Figure 17

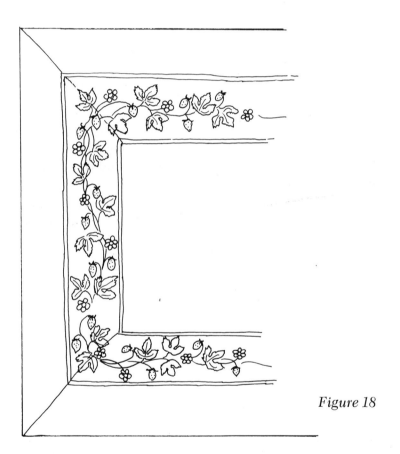

Figure 18

When choosing your wools, be sure that they match as closely as possible the colors of the design to be re-created or blend harmoniously with the color scheme in your room.

A wealth of border ideas surround one in the trimming departments of fabric stores (Plates 20 and 21). However, I have also found that many of the ones I chose to reproduce on canvas did not lend themselves to the confinement of the canvas and had to be cajoled for more hours of experimentation than I had planned on.

Christmas Tree with appliquéd toys and packages. Braided rug and paneled walls make up a unique border effect. Designed and worked by Betty Bohannon.

One very important thing to remember is that some fabric designs expand greatly when applied to canvas. Occasionally, one gets so large that it no longer falls into the realm of a border pattern. If you stitch your border on a finer mesh, 18 instead of 14 for instance, it becomes easier to reproduce and your end result will be more in proportion to your material (Plate 20 versus Plate 21).

Coordinating your border with your central design takes a great deal of imagination and planning. It should definitely be put on the canvas before you take the first stitch, either in outline or totally painted in.

To incorporate your border into your central design may be difficult as the design may not lend itself to this. Two instances where it has been worked out effectively, however, are the Railroad Scene (Plate 22) where the railroad track becomes the border, and the Peaceful Lion (Plate 23) encompassed by fish and stream.

Sometimes it is fun to research a border in terms of central design. The Game Bird Rug (Plate 24), for example, has been done in six squares, each bordered with a garland depicting the leaves and berries which each of these six birds eat. The three woodland creatures, owl, fawn, and rabbit (Plate 25), are enclosed with sophisticated borders, each depicting that animal's habitat or plumage. The possibilities of coordinating borders such as these are endless.

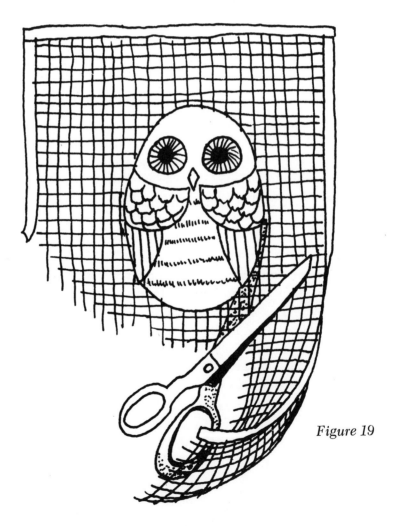

Figure 19

Mounting to Create a Border

Often you will find that it takes much longer to complete a piece of needlepoint than you had anticipated. When lack of time dictates that you are not able to add a border, then there are mounting techniques that can make up for it and give your finished piece the illusion of having a border.

Pillows

When you want to mount your completed project as a pillow, there are several options open to you, depending on whether you want a light, airy effect or a more sophisticated one. If your sewing skills are not above average, however, I strongly recommend that you take your project to a professional mounter. It would be a shame to have your hours of creativity ruined by careless mounting.

Ready-Made Pillow with Braid

One of the simplest ways to finish a small piece is to buy a ready-made pillow. Find one that complements the color scheme and texture of your needlework. It need not be a solid color as verified in Plate 26 where the Owl design is set onto a gay plaid.

Cut the unstitched canvas to within 1½″ of the stitched area (Figure 19) and turn under 1½″ of unstitched canvas plus one or two rows of the stitched area. Slip-stitch the entire piece to your pillow. To cover the edges of your design attach a piece of braid or ribbon. Stretchy braid works best and it eliminates the need for mitering. Tack it on all the way around. Do not cut

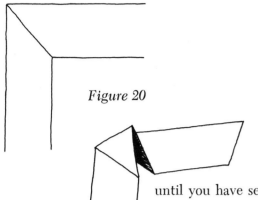

Figure 20

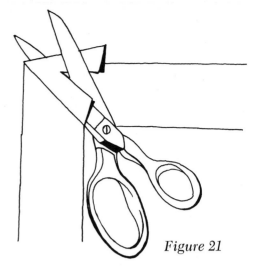

Figure 21

BACK

until you have sewn around to the last corner. Cut, leaving enough excess to turn under so that it won't ravel.

Mitered Ribbon

A pretty ribbon applied to the edges of a piece of needlework can create a very effective border (Plate 2). When using ribbon or braid that needs mitering, lay the right side of the ribbon to the right side of the needlework and pin the edges. When the sides are aligned, take the pins out except at the corners. Carefully fold the corners to make a miter (Figure 20). Cut off the excess material (Figure 21) and sew the corners. After sewing all four corners, sew the sides.

To apply braid on top of the mitered ribbon (Plate 27) or material, use one long uncut piece of braid. Pin it in place. Sew it on with enough ease to round the corners softly. At the end leave enough braid, about ½″, to turn under and overlap your beginning (Figure 22).

Inserting

To insert a piece of needlepoint into fabric so that the fabric itself becomes the border, cut four pieces of fabric the length and width you want the front of your pillow to be (Figure 23). Place the right side of the fabric to the right sides of the needlepoint. Sew all around. Miter the corners. Cut off any excess fabric to ⅜″. Fold flat sideways. Turn the fabric to the right side and press flat. Topstitch the mitered corners (Figure 24). The front of your pillow is now ready.

Figure 22

Inserting Ruffles

Ruffles on a knife-edged or boxed pillow create a light and airy effect (Plate 28). This is done by cutting your fabric on the bias or straight, twice the desired width of your ruffle plus seam allowance. Cut enough fabric for two and one-half times the circumference of the pillow. Gather by machine or hand.

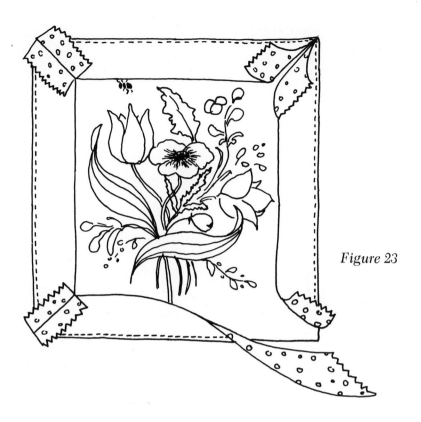

Figure 23

Figure 24

Place the front and back of the pillow together with the right sides of the fabric facing each other. Sandwich the ruffle between them, with the actual ruffle facing toward the center (Figure 25). Stitch all three pieces together on three sides. *Stitch the ruffle to the front piece only on the fourth side*, leaving the back piece free so the pillow can be stuffed. After stuffing, slip-stitch the fourth side closed.

It might be pointed out here that eyelet and other materials can be purchased in two ways: flat or preruffled. The latter will certainly save you a great deal of time, provided a suitable one is applied. If you do use a preruffled fabric, purchase enough for the circumference of your pillow plus a bit extra for overlap.

The ribbon in Plate 29 was attached according to the mitered ribbon directions. A bow with long ends was then attached to the corner and tacked on. Gather or loop the long ends and tack.

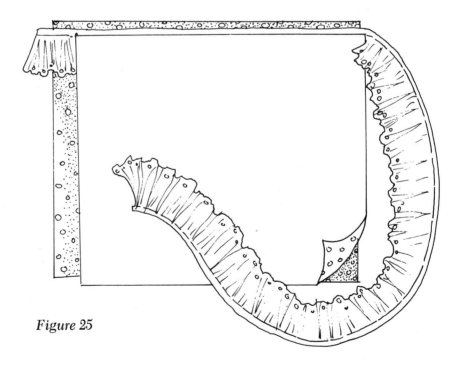

Figure 25

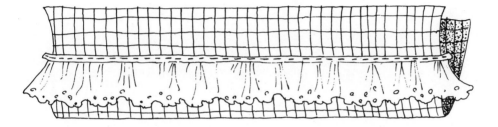

Figure 26

Applying Gathered Eyelet to a Ruffled Fabric

This can be difficult but the result is pretty and frilly, particularly for something like a boudoir pillow (Plate 29). To apply your pregathered eyelet to fabric which has been cut for a ruffle, first sew the eyelet to the straight ruffle fabric (Figure 26).

After sewing the eyelet on, gather the fabric softly to create a ruffle. Attach it to the front of the pillow using the method described for inserting ruffles on pages 88–90. Fold back on the top and the front of the pillow and pin it out of the way so that you will not get it caught in the seams as you are completing the pillow. This pillow can be made boxed or knife-edged.

If boxed, as in Plate 29, measure the size of the needlepoint plus any border material, adding 1½″ for seam allowance. Cut a piece of backing material the same dimensions. To cut boxing, measure the circumference of your pillow plus 1½″ at each end for turn-under. Cut one strip of fabric this length and the desired width, always allowing 1½″ each side for seam.

Place the right side of the boxing material against the right side of the needlepoint. Stitch all around. Turn right side out and press gently, especially at the corners. Place the right side of the back material to the right side of the boxing and stitch on three sides only, *leaving the fourth side open for stuffing.* After stuffing, slip-stitch the fourth side closed.

Two pillows mounted using the insert with mitered-corner technique. Designed and worked by Judy Zachs.

Weaving colored ribbons through the holes in the eyelet ruffle adds another bit of color (Plate 28). Tie bows where the different colors meet at the corners and the center sides.

The best materials to use for stuffing are polyethylene or dacron polyester. There are also many sizes of fiber-filled forms which are labor- and time-saving conveniences, but be sure your form is the correct size for your needlepoint or it will have an understuffed look and shortly lose its shape. Foam rubber can also be used, but it gives the piece a very rigid appearance and, if it collects moisture, has been known to rot needlepoint.

I have barely skimmed the surface of border-creating effects for mounting a pillow. A little needle know-how combined with the use of your imagination will turn your pillows into conversation pieces.

Stitchery Framing

A frame can become the border for many pieces of needlework. One cannot overemphasize the importance of proper framing for needlework. Framing should never be chosen for price alone; if framed incorrectly your piece can be ruined.

First of all, leave at least 1½ to 2″ outside the design area. This is necessary for proper blocking and stretching.

Many framers do not wish to do blocking and if this is the case in your area, and you are not proficient in this technique yourself, take your piece to your local needlework shop and have a professional block it for you. Too often people try to do their own blocking to save money, and finish up with scalloping on the edges of the design; this is called mooning.

Techniques have been developed to avoid numerous pitfalls of mounting. Some pieces are covered with picture or glare-free glass. This now tends to be avoided with needlework, however, because moisture that gets under the glass will cause a piece to mildew. If glass is used it should never rest upon the needlework itself.

The majority of pieces framed without glass are now padded with a very thin layer of synthetic material, carried by most framers. This padding

Mirror Frame
employing a simple
stitched border.
Stitched by
Judy Zachs.

eliminates the wavy look caused by stretching over a period of time and gives an added dimension to the work.

The selection of the frame is of prime importance, and your final decision will generally be influenced by the shape and design of the work itself, or its future location.

You can create a border effect by applying the technique of a double frame (Plate 30). Here the patron saint of needlework, St. Clare, is bordered by a dainty wood frame, then a border of velvet, then a more elaborate wood frame which picks up the blue of her robe.

A round piece of needlepoint could be set in a matting of suitable fabric, then framed with an octagonal frame. This type of frame may be hard to find and may have to be custom-made, but the end result will be a spectacular one to be handed down through many generations. Antique shops, flea markets, and junk stores are often wonderful places to find frames that are no longer available commercially.

Graphs for Samplers

Spider Web

Form eight-point star. Now wind thread under and over each arm as many times as necessary. This stitch can be made larger or smaller, according to the size of the star.

Plate 5, Figure 2, Set 1

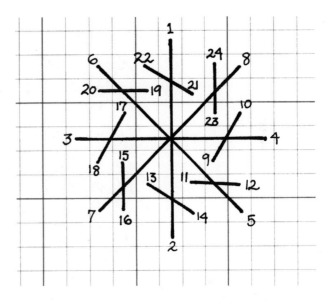

Diagonal Leaf

A center vein can be added to this stitch if desired. It can also be made larger or smaller by adding or subtracting side stitches.

Plate 5, Figure 2, Set 1

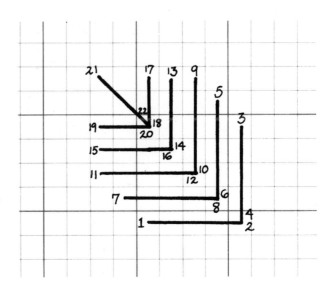

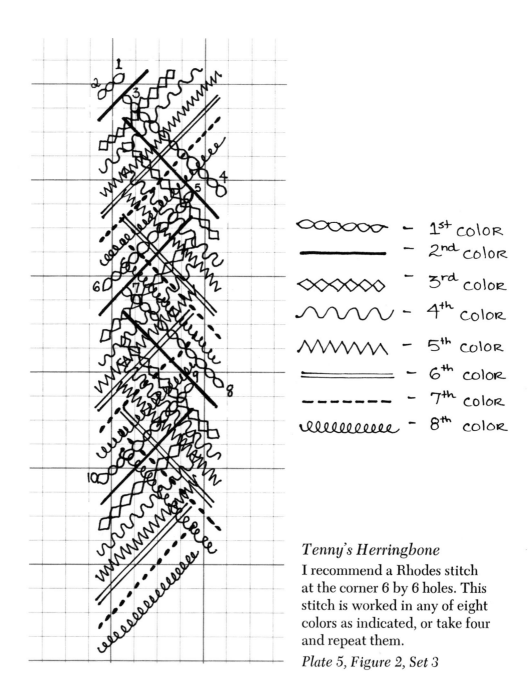

∞∞∞∞∞∞	– 1st color
——————	– 2nd color
⬦⬦⬦⬦⬦	– 3rd color
∿∿∿∿∿	– 4th color
∧∧∧∧∧∧	– 5th color
══════	– 6th color
– – – – –	– 7th color
ℓℓℓℓℓℓℓℓℓ	– 8th color

Tenny's Herringbone

I recommend a Rhodes stitch at the corner 6 by 6 holes. This stitch is worked in any of eight colors as indicated, or take four and repeat them.

Plate 5, Figure 2, Set 3

Diagonal Brick

This stitch done on the diagonal covers better than when done straight up and down.

Plate 5, Figure 2, Sets 4 and 12

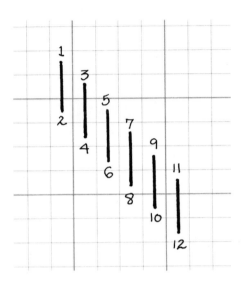

Shadow Mesh

Done in three colors, this can be a very effective stitch.

Plate 12, Figure 9, Set 10

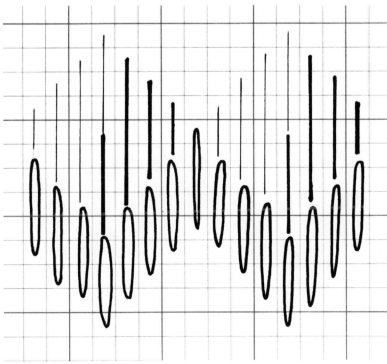

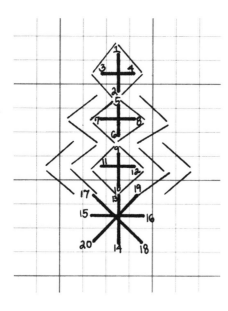

Christmas Tree
Slanted stitches with upright cross in the centers and Smyrna cross at the base.

Plate 5, Figure 2, Set 4

Milanese
Best worked in sharply contrasting colors.
Forms tiny Christmas-tree-like figures.

Plate 5, Figure 2, Set 12

Plate 12, Figure 9, Set 1

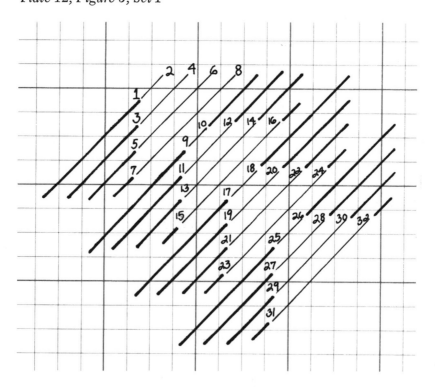

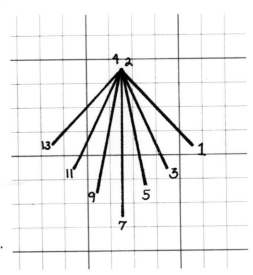

Diamond Ray
Even numbers all enter same hole.
Plate 12, Figure 9, Set 11

Double Star
Do center first, then surround with flat
stitches.
Plate 12, Figure 9, Set 2

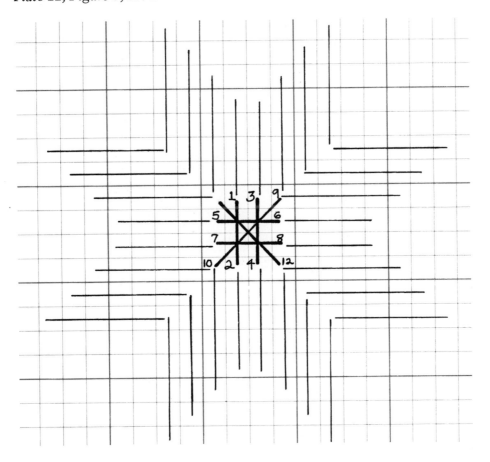

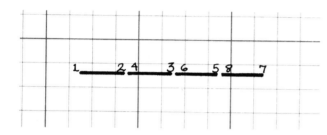

Backstitch

Useful to fill in any space where the canvas shows.

Plate 12, Figure 9, Set 8

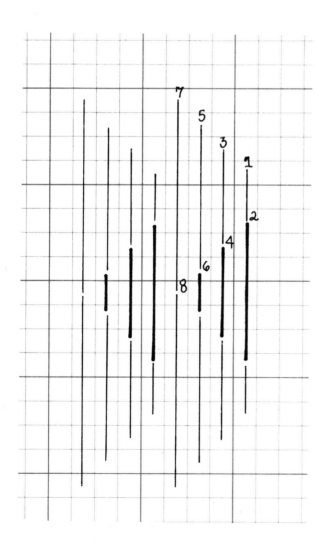

Van Dyke

Straight stitches which can be done in two contrasting colors.

Plate 7, Figure 4, Set 4

Long-Armed Cross

One cross is up three holes and over three holes while the other is up three holes and over five.

Plate 7, Figure 4, Set 9

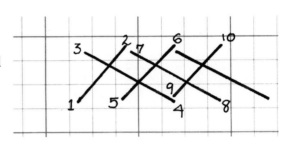

Banded Cross

Large X whose arms are crossed in both diagonal directions.

Plate 12, Figure 9, Set 4

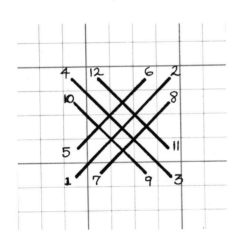

Montenegrin

A variation of the long-armed cross. 3, 5, and 7 share a common hole; 6–10 also share a common hole.

Plate 5, Figure 2, Set 9

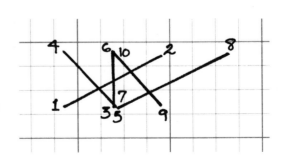

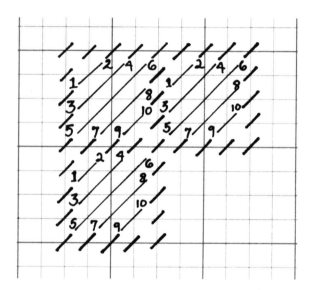

Scotch Stitch

This stitch has many variations. As shown here it is surrounded with tent stitch.

Plate 5, Figure 2, Set 10

Plate 7, Figure 4, Sets 2 and 6

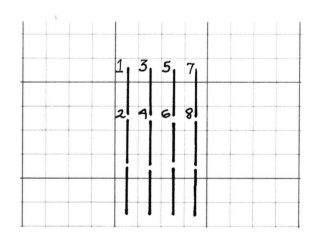

Straight Gobelin

Likely to show the background of the canvas, so it is advisable to paint canvas the color of your yarn.

Plate 5, Figure 2, Set 12

Plate 7, Figure 4, Set 6

Plate 12, Figure 9, Sets 7 and 8

Plate 5, Figure 2, Set 12

Plate 6

This stitch changes as it goes around the corner. Note difference in two sides.

Diamond Eyelet

Odd numbers starting with 1 are in center
hole. Worked over five holes, 4, 3, 2, and
five holes again using the same center
hole. A running or backstitch may be used
as outline.

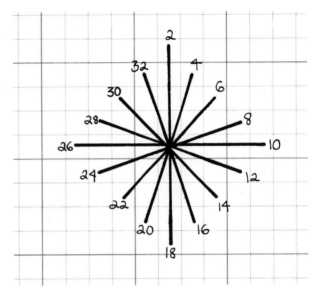

Rosemary

Can often be used instead of Hungarian.
A lovely pattern stitch.

Plate 5, Figure 2, Set 9

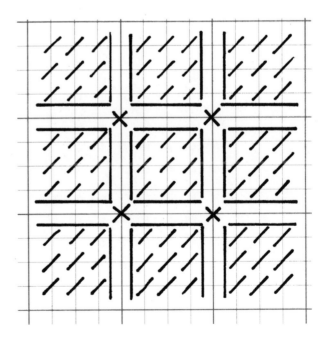

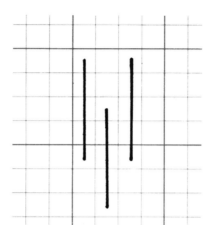

Duck's Feet
Can be done by alternating colors; the sets
fit in one above the other.
Plate 5, Figure 2, Set 7

Ribbon Stitch
The end result of this stitch really gives the
appearance of ribbon. Tent stitches
surround flat stitches.
Plate 5, Figure 2, Set 8

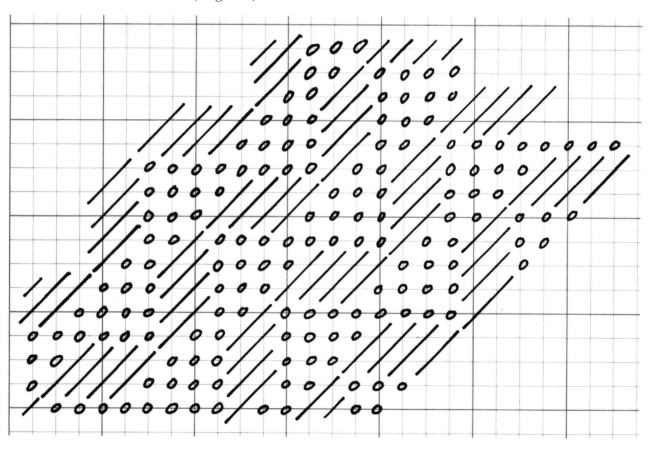

Oblong Cross

Simply an elongated cross-stitch. The top
stitches should always slant to the right.
It may be tied down with a backstitch as
indicated by numbers 5 and 6.

Plate 5, Figure 2, Set 5

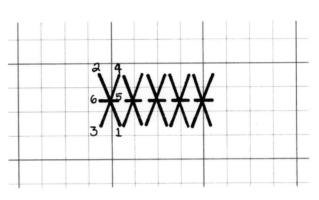

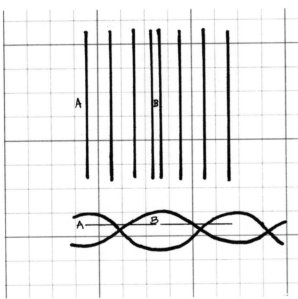

Shell Stitch

Two groups of four stitches share a
common hole. Each set of four stitches is
tied down. Thread of contrasting color is
threaded spirally twice through the back
stitches.

Plate 5, Figure 2, Set 5

Slanting Gobelin

Really an oblong tent stitch, up three holes
and over one. It may be used anywhere.

Plate 5, Figure 2, Set 12

Plate 7, Figure 4, Sets 2 and 6

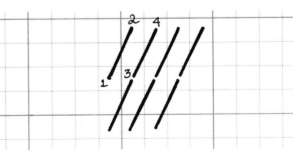

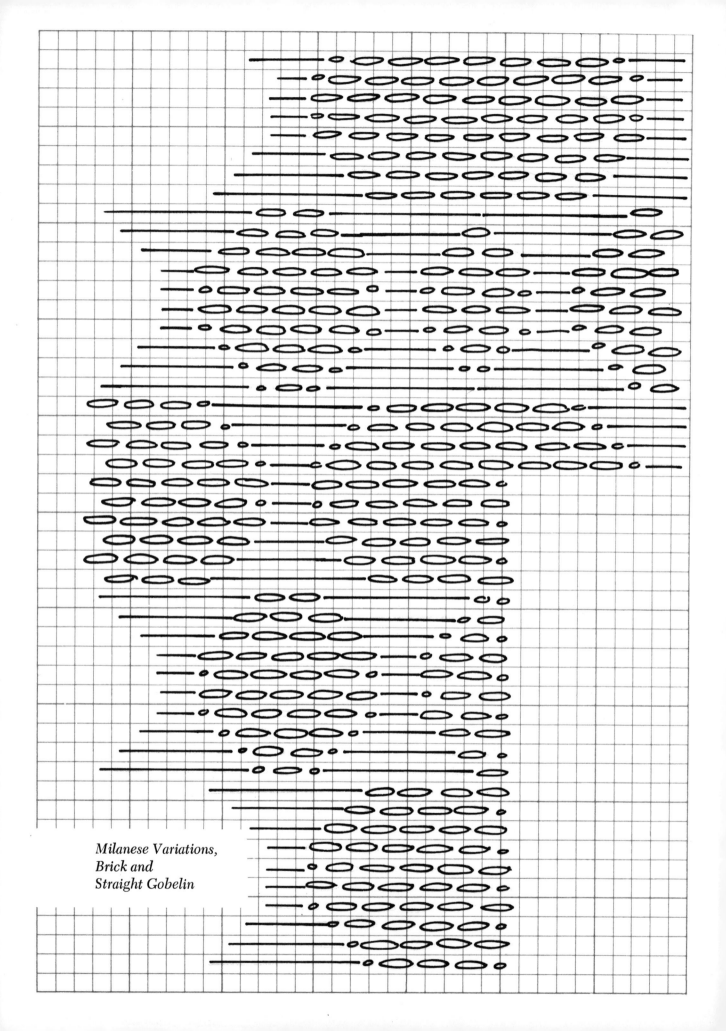

*Milanese Variations,
Brick and
Straight Gobelin*

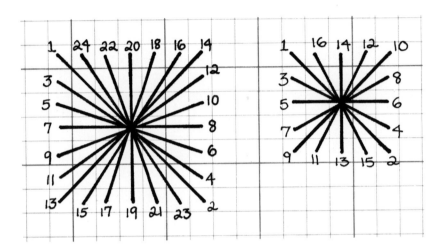

Rhodes Stitch

Bring needle up on odd numbers,
down on even. May be adapted
to any size square.

Plate 5, Figure 2, Set 3

Turkey Knot

Begin on front of canvas.

Step 1. Needle down at A, up at B, down at
C, up at A; pull tightly.

Step 2. Needle down at D, leave loop. Up at
E, down at F, up at D; pull tightly.

Step 3. Needle down at G, leave loop, up at
H, down at I, up at G; pull tightly.

Continue in this fashion. Start each new row
at the bottom and work to the top. Loops may
be cut for a "furry pile."

Plate 8

On the following pages you can try making your own designs.

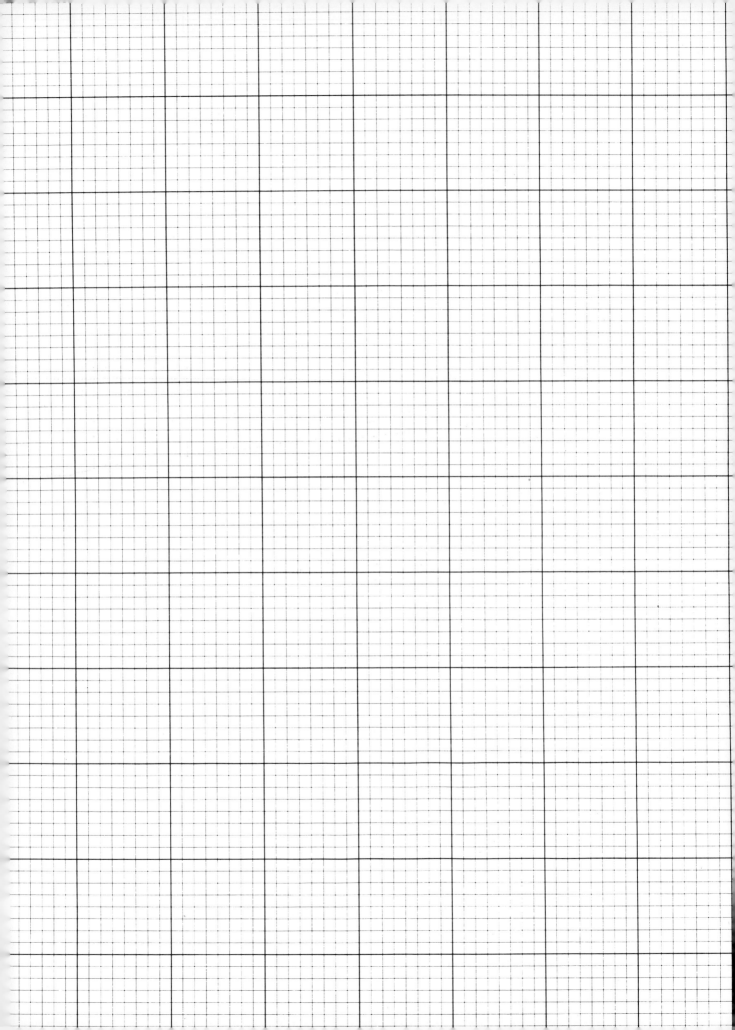

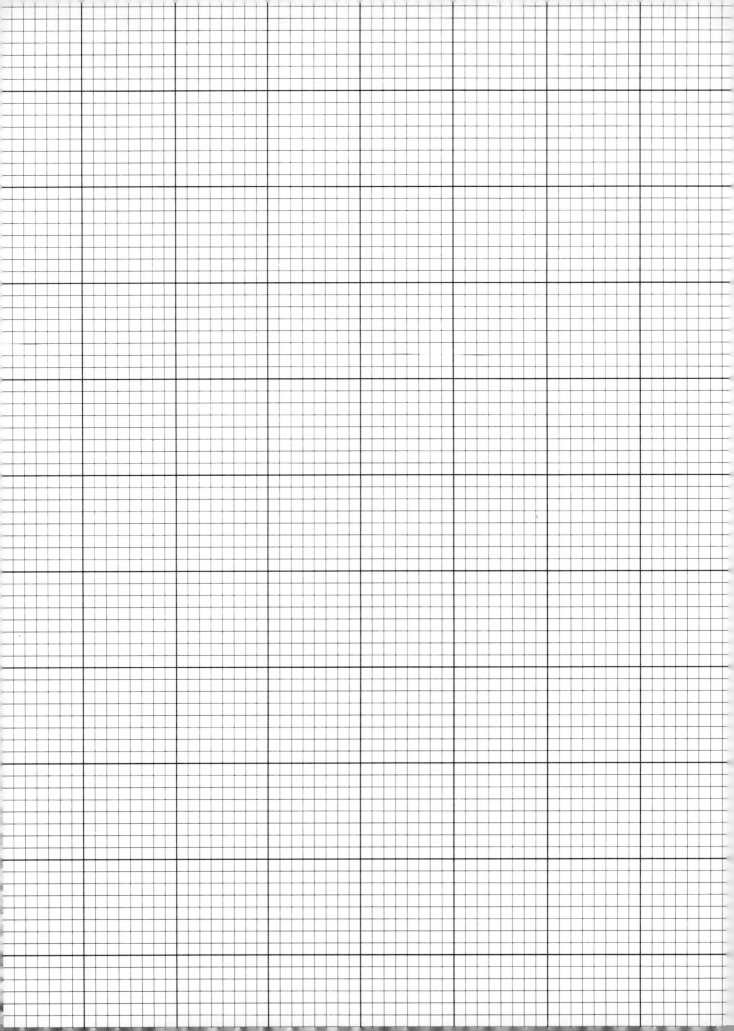

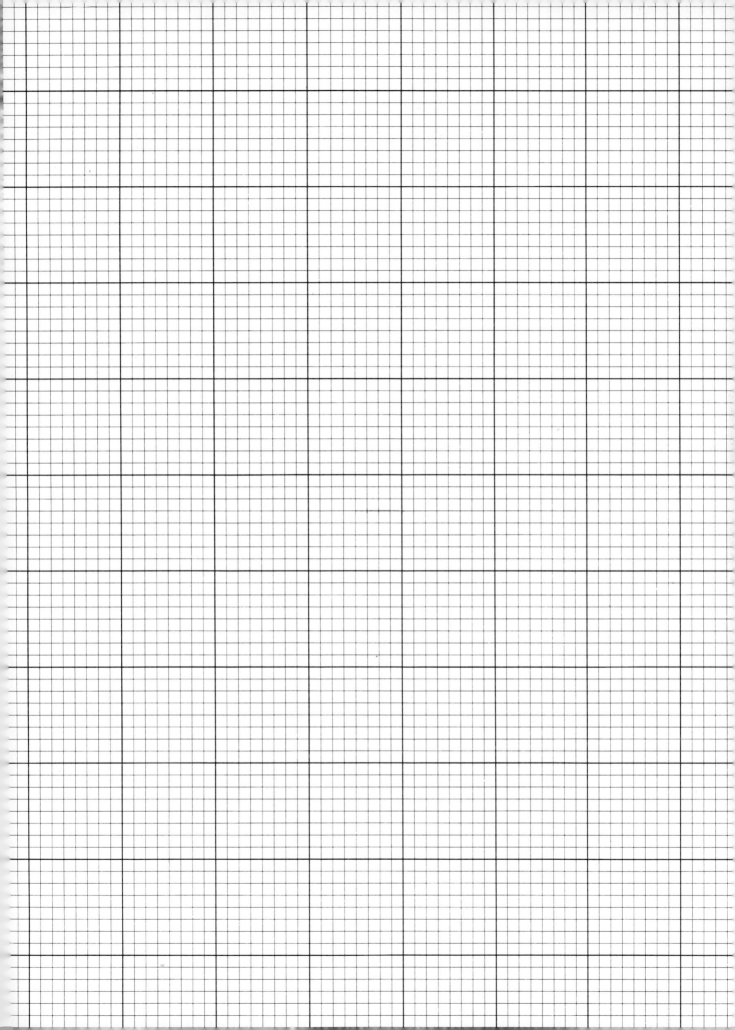

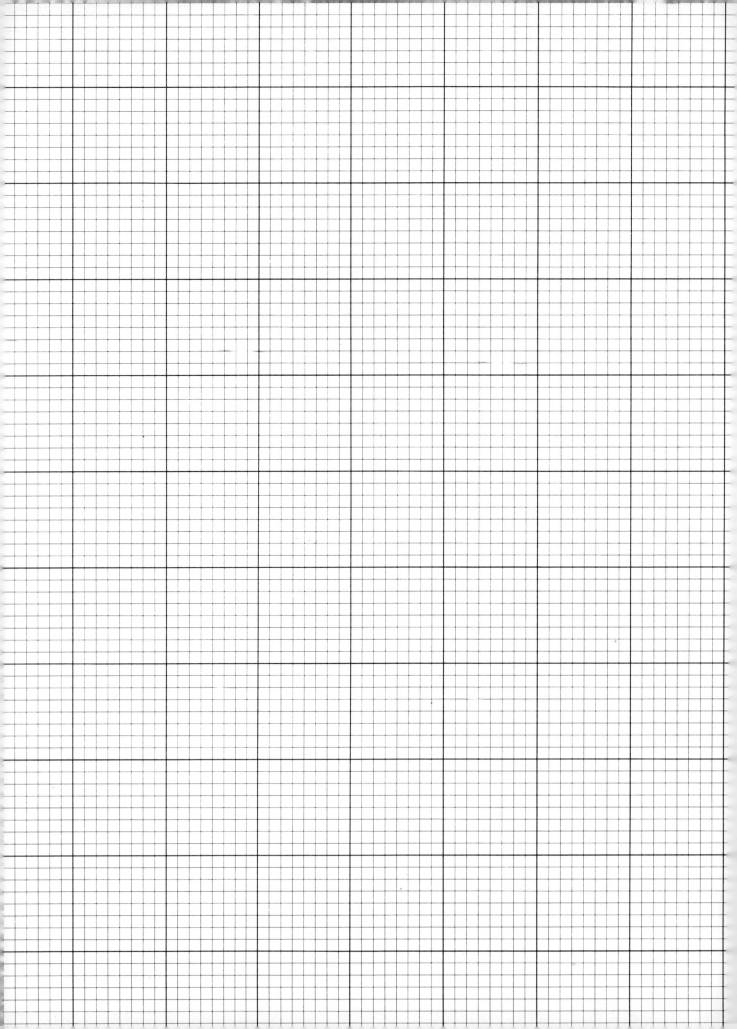